*Older
but Better,
but Older*

OLDER
but
BETTER,
but
OLDER

*

CAROLINE DE MAIGRET
AND SOPHIE MAS

EBURY
PRESS

3 5 7 9 10 8 6 4 2

First published by Ebury Press in 2020

Ebury Press an imprint of Ebury Publishing,
20 Vauxhall Bridge Road, London SW1V 2SA

Ebury Press is part of the Penguin Random House group of companies
whose addresses can be found at global.penguinrandomhouse.com

Copyright © 2020 Caroline de Maigret, Sophie Mas, Anne Berest and
Audrey Diwan

This is a translation of the unpublished French manuscript, copyright ©
2020 by Caroline de Maigret, Sophie Mas, Anne Berest and Audrey Diwan

English translation copyright © 2020
by Susanna Lea Associates

Caroline de Maigret, Sophie Mas, Anne Berest and Audrey Diwan
have asserted their right to be identified as the authors of this work in
accordance with the Copyright, Designs and Patents Act 1988

First published in the United States by Doubleday, a division of Random
House LLC, New York

www.penguin.co.uk

A CIP catalogue record for this book is available from the British Library

ISBN 9781529104486

Printed and bound in Italy by L.E.G.O. S.p.A.

The L.C. Smith 5 Typewriter font used on pages 23, 65, 79, 95, 145, 159,
191 and 205 courtesy of Dr. Georg Sommergger (typewriters.ch).

MIX
Paper from
responsible sources
FSC
www.fsc.org   FSC® C018179

Penguin Random House is committed to a
sustainable future for our business, our readers
and our planet. This book is made from Forest
Stewardship Council® certified paper.

'Age is something that doesn't matter,

unless you are a cheese.'

—LUIS BUÑUEL

Older
but Better,
but Older

YOU KNOW THINGS AREN'T WHAT THEY USED TO BE

When you wake up feeling great and everyone tells you how tired you look.

When you go to see the dermatologist to check a mole and he asks where you want the Botox.

When a thirty-year-old guy arrives at a party and doesn't even glance at you.

When you can guess from his personality what kind of a lover he is.

When the President of France is younger than you.

When you have more hangovers than actual parties.

When in all honesty you'd rather have sex in bed than in the shower.

When you go to the gym to do cardio, and no longer just to work on your abs.

When you find yourself putting on makeup every day.

When you think you look good in a photo of yourself at twenty that until now you'd always thought was terrible.

When you no longer know who all the hip actors or singers are.

When someone says you have a sexy gaze, but you're actually just squinting because you don't want to get your glasses out.

When you tell someone you've known them since they were in nappies.

When you share an anecdote from ten years ago and realise it's actually been twenty.

When you'd rather go to bed early to make the most of the next day.

When you start finding biographies fascinating.

When you're just excited to go home.

When your colleague was born the same year you graduated.

When people no longer ask if you plan on having another baby.

When a young woman says she hopes to look like you someday.

When you go to the ob-gyn for mammograms rather than birth control.

When you feel an ache somewhere and fear it might be the beginning of the end.

When one of your eyes is smaller than the other.

When selecting your year of birth on a website means scrolling down forever.

When the face ID on your mobile phone doesn't recognise you in the morning.

When you're told that you're 'damn hot for your age'.

When you smile at the naïveté of a young woman's remark, whereas before you would have just found her stupid.

When you think that's a pillow mark on your cheek, but it's still there a week later.

Your
First

You used to live for firsts. First kiss, dry lips and pounding heart. First salary – a sum so tiny it vanished in three nights. Your first time clubbing, caked in makeup, trying to fool them at the door, trembling at the thought they'd see right through you. The first dubious fling you brought home to your baffled but sympathetic parents. That disturbing film you saw alone in a dark cinema, and the first time you took the highway by yourself, feverish at the wheel. Your first time filing taxes and feeling serious, a true adult. The first time you got dumped when you didn't see it coming, and then got over it – to your surprise. Or when you lost your virginity and nothing really changed. First night alone in your first flat . . . Moments of joy, sadness and adrenaline that marked the end or the beginning of new eras. You think back with affection on these moments that made you grow. And though your firsts are rarer now, they still happen. They take on new forms, more complex shapes.

When you found your first grey hair some years ago, it strangely didn't affect you much because some of your friends had them at twenty-five.

But this first time fills you with stupor and with dread. It hits you instantly when you catch it, making eyes at you. A solitary white hair hiding in your pubes. It's not a mirage as you first hoped. You double-check, give it a tug – it's definitely there and not going anywhere. It's all you can see, smugly soaking up attention, taunting you. **Is this even normal?** You're not prepared for this, not yet. You know some parts of you won't stay the same forever and it's all part of the game, but this first you wanted nothing to do with.

Just as you're about to drown in your own misery, you remember that blondish-whitish eyebrow hair that you've had since age fifteen. You know it well. It grows back from time to time, always coarse, always alone, pale, in that very same spot on the left side of the arch, unpigmented. There's never been another one like it – until now. If this new counterpart asserts its independence, you're ready to let it be. As long as he stays single.

You think back with affection on these moments that made you grow.

The
Second
Love of
Your Life

- He may not be Leonardo DiCaprio – but he doesn't ghost you after your first date.

  - **You didn't grow up in the same country – yet you speak the same language.**

- He's not at all what you had imagined, but luckily reality beats fiction.

  - **He doesn't have a lot of hair, but he has a lot of words in his vocabulary.**

- He didn't spend his youth trying to catch the perfect wave, but he did read *The Old Man and the Sea*.

  - **He can't sprint to catch the bus, but he knows all the best shortcuts.**

- He already has several children. Great – so do you.

YOU KNOW THINGS AREN'T
WHAT THEY USED TO BE

WHEN IN ALL HONESTY YOU'D RATHER HAVE SEX IN BED THAN IN THE SHOWER.

WHO SAID MEN AGE MORE GRACEFULLY?

You're having dinner with your old high school buddies, a group of people you adore but see only once every two years, which is the time it takes for everyone to coordinate their schedules.

You feel good, you rediscover the smiling faces, the caring looks and funny anecdotes.

And suddenly, looking around the table and taking a step back, you're struck by something: the beauty of the women surrounding you. They've all had their struggles and their victories. They've all been through different ordeals. But what they all have in common is trying to keep up a certain idea of their bodies, of their seductiveness . . . an image of themselves that they like.

But the men? It's a different story . . .

As you look at them, you slowly see the truth behind the line that everyone, men and women, buys into: like a good wine, men supposedly get better with age. We say silver foxes are appealing. We repeat that their wrinkles are a measure of their experience, and make them even sexier. That their love handles are disarming and therefore charming. So obviously, why would they make an effort? After all, why not . . . except that some of them confuse being a silver fox with a dicey haircut, crow's-feet with a dubious complexion and a few extra pounds with a beer belly.

Faced with this supposed injustice and forced to believe they've already lost the battle, women do twice as much as the opposite sex to look good. Weirdly enough, if we consider reality from another angle, and dismantle our assumptions – women do age well, if not better.

BEST BEFORE

I t was a routine visit, the checkup she went for every year, more or less, with the enthusiasm of a trip to the DMV: mammogram, smear test, blood pressure, weight *and are your periods all okay?* This time around, the conversation veered into intimate territory.

Do you want children?

She didn't come with the intention of discussing her life with her gynaecologist but hears herself answering as though from her therapist's couch (instead of legs spread wide in stirrups) that, yes, she'd like to be a mother one day, but for now she's single with no immediate plans to have a baby on her own.

The clock is ticking.

Silence. The words linger heavily in the room.

Have you considered freezing your eggs?

And that's how her future was decided, stamped with an expiration date. Gone were the days of 'It's fine, you've got time.' This was a tacit 'What were you doing all these years?' or, crueller still, 'Here's one who thinks she's a man.'

If she was honest with herself, she *did* think that. Her grandmother had earned the right to vote; her mother, sexual freedom and contraception, divorce and abortions; and she (or so she thought) had earned the same rights as the opposite sex. To not depend on anyone. For success without guilt. To have a child – on her own terms.

This wasn't denial, but a desire – as with everything else (her job, her independence) – to make goals a reality. Yes, I can. It was simple: she hadn't found the right person yet, was finally getting to know herself and stabilise everything she'd built so far. A baby? Later. She was young, fit, got through thirty minutes on the elliptical without spitting up a lung. Pregnancy? Later! How many women had their first child in their forties? She had enough examples in mind to not worry about the stats.

A bunch of trivial words interrupt her thoughts: the gynaecologist is prattling on about protocol, hormones, activation, treatments, needles, operations. What?! As she seeks refuge on a chair that suddenly feels so big, she grasps (despite herself) what this man is saying. Fertility drops after thirty-five, so many couples can't 'get pregnant' . . . but also, the thought of buying time.

She'd never considered freezing eggs. At least not her own. She couldn't shake the stupid image of a carton in the fridge. There was no poetry there – anticipating, measuring, safekeeping . . . Wasn't love precisely the opposite? A chance encounter, an act of magic, unpredictable and spontaneous. She is definitely the product of a traditional upbringing, raised on another century's beliefs (the twentieth, as it were). The doctor suggests she think on it and book a new appointment if she wants to begin the process, although he warns her that just freezing her eggs does not guarantee they will be fertile.

Back on the street she fumbles for her keys, battling with her purse and starting her car so she can get back to life as she left it an hour ago.

* * *

Should she discuss it or keep quiet? She tests it out in conversation over the next few days, and discovers a fierce taboo on the topic. It threatens the so-called feminine mystique (no, a woman has neither organs nor biological problems, only the power to make life appear between her legs), it touches on the shame or fear of failing in this domain especially, of being single, of missing the optimal fertility window (the capitalistic imperative to perform has snuck into our bedrooms).

Soon around her, tongues start to loosen, conflicting opinions crystallise. Some have saved up and secretly done it already, others think the process is unnatural, others yet are just afraid. In the end she decides alone.

She summons her courage and, prescription in hand, collects her ovary-stimulation kit from the pharmacy. It's a little confusing and intimidating, but she gets the gist: it all begins with her next cycle.

The first day of her period is the first day of a completely new experience. It marks a new relationship with her body: She is, literally, taking matters into her own hands. As she pinches her lower abdomen, inserts the minuscule syringe, realises she can actually do it and that the pain is bearable – it feels like a first victory. She knows that she will see this through. Above all, she's grateful for this mottled collection of tissues, veins, organs and cells that make up who she is and will accept what she's about to ask of them.

Twenty days later. The small, impersonal waiting rooms at the fertility clinic have tinted windows so that people don't run into one another. Shame is strong when you step outside the norm. She keeps her eyes down and shyly makes her way through. Then things move quickly: the operation is over in thirty minutes, the post-anesthesia wake-up is hazy, and then comes a feeling of triumph at vanquishing her fears: she now has nine eggs frozen in liquid nitrogen. It's so simple. Yet she feels punctured all over, there's a tsunami raging under her skin and in her heart. She feels like something vital has been taken from her, a part of her DNA gone.

* * *

Over the next few days she is hit by steady pangs of sadness, but she feels freer too. Her hormones are in free fall and she has many questions, but she knows it's a new start. More than a medical procedure, this operation feels like a reboot, a software update to self-actualisation. There is no fear anymore as she explores her own desires and the questions they might prompt. Does she really want a child? Could she raise it alone if she doesn't find the right person?

As her busy life takes over again, she realises that she's given herself a gift, an incredible essential thing: a new option. And some extra time to fall in love, for the *right* reasons instead of rushing for the sake of it. That ticking clock with its terrifying power no longer scares her. The *tick-tock* that echoes across our bodies like a time bomb is gone. With a lightness in her heart she thinks about her microscopic little eggs, crystals of herself stocked in pearly vials at $-196°$ Celsius, happy at the thought that the unknown can enter the realm of possibilities again.

YOU KNOW THINGS AREN'T
WHAT THEY USED TO BE

**When you think
that's a pillow mark
on your cheek,
but it's still there
a week later.**

THE
CATCH-22s

White wine gives you palpitations	Red wine gives you stained teeth
A few extra pounds on your backside	A few extra wrinkles on your gaunt face
Running and dying from knee pain	Doing yoga and dying of boredom
A young Madam	An old Miss
Hanging out with a younger guy and looking like a cougar	Hanging out with an older one and looking like you have a sugar daddy
Getting home after midnight	Getting up before 8 a.m.
Opting for SPF 70 and a pasty face	Opting for a tan and crow's-feet
Damaging your hair with dye	Accepting white hair that damages your self-esteem
Trying not to look like your mother	Accepting that you've already become your mother

THAT
EXTRA
SOMETHING

The second you got to the party, you couldn't take your eyes off him. There he was, handsome and proud, surrounded by enraptured friends. You'd never seen him before and you liked him instantly. His aura projected you immediately into your future life together. You could picture the scene: a summer evening in a little house in the south of France, sitting around a wooden table reinventing the world, drunk on rosé. The children tucked up in bed, the air still warm.

He caught you watching, came over to talk, you laughed, you drank, you liked each other, he kissed you, and finished the night at yours.

You hadn't felt this good with a man in ages. Everything feels right, the way he touches you, intense with almost loving tenderness. He thinks you're beautiful, flatters you just enough, whispers sweet words already, so soon. When he talks about himself it's never too much, he spares you the banalities of daily life and tells you only epic tales. This man lives in the moment like no other, so different from guys you've been with recently, predictable neurotic types who don't know what they want. In fact, what he wants never comes up – he's above all that, serene, assured. He desires you more than anything, sends you passionate messages at lunchtime, wants you now, immediately, only to disappear and reappear as he pleases, which drives you crazy – with love.

You like the mystery surrounding him. You don't know much, his online presence is purely professional and you have no friends in common. As far as you know. You wonder if Pierre, the childhood friend who brought you to that party, knows more. You call him and meet up at the café downstairs. You tell him all about your love affair, your bliss at finally finding a man at ease in his own skin, how this time, you think, it might be for real. Turns out, when you meet the right person everything's so easy! You'll have to remember that for next time (if there ever is a next time), that there's no point holding on if it doesn't feel exactly right. Either he's the one or he's not. You see, Pierre, this guy has something extra you can't define, and it makes all the difference.

Pierre blushes, looks down at his feet, and tells you gently: *'You're right, honey, he does have an extra something, and quite a something it is. It's called a wife and two kids.'*

Owning Your Insecurities

don't like my butt. I just don't. I've disliked it since the summer I was seventeen, when a guy accosted me at the club to inform me that my bum hung low.

I didn't know him, he was probably wasted, or another jerk whose main pickup technique was to prey on our insecurities. Strategically positioning himself as the only guy at the party who could *possibly* be into a body as strange as mine. Wasn't I lucky to find such a generous, open-minded catch?

His words had done their damage. I had finally solved the mystery of what went on behind me, the view accessible to all but myself. That lightheartedness that had the audacity to stroll around would now have to sit itself right down.

The next morning I developed a specially tailored trick for the beach. A kind of crab-walk crossed with surprising pelvic movements, to get from beach towel to the sea. I still perform this ludicrous dance, convinced it prevents a clear sight of my behind.

One September morning a few weeks later the fateful question arose: what to wear for the first day of sixth form? I had a gravity problem to fix.

I had no baggy trousers, so I raided my brother's wardrobe. I found a pair of tailored brown trousers that I hiked all the way up, tightly fastened with a belt. For the top I borrowed a white shirt, worn with an extra button undone so I could resemble Katharine Hepburn, whose modern elegance had always inspired me. The outfit nailed its primary purpose – and it wasn't half bad. At school, friends praised my new look.

It was my first time grappling with the concept of a look, of style and allure. I began to understand the value of pushing a detail a little further for a more interesting overall result: these weren't just wide trousers that hid what I disliked. These trousers gave me a devil-may-care, original nonchalance. From a constraint, I had crafted a flattering style that I liked.

But I still can't believe a nightclub loser helped me find it.

These trousers gave me
a devil-may-care,
original nonchalance.

You Still Forget, Every Time,

…that it's a bad idea to plan on working while on holiday.

…**what your alcohol tolerance is. You're still convinced that you can handle yourself five glasses in.**

…that a trip with your in-laws for a week is far too much; in fact, so is a weekend.

…**that new love stories come with baggage: workaholism, travel, sometimes even an ex-wife and kids.**

…that you have to pick your battles. You can't get hung up on everything that bugs you.

…**that happiness is a discipline. It comes from you.**

... that you're about to get your period and that's probably why you're cranky.

... that you should only look in the mirror under good lighting – what matters is how you feel, not how you look.

... that when your love life is a mess, it's still better than boredom.

... that working out is vital for your mind.

... and you still forget, every time, when Mr Arsehole calls you, why you named him that in your Contacts. And then you remember.

MAKEUP TIPS

The good thing about time passing is that you learn what suits you. You master the colours and materials that flatter you, you have a favourite brand of blush or under-eye concealer. You used to think that, once acquired, this knowledge would last forever. But you hadn't factored in your age. Every day your skin gets a little looser, your outlines a little blurrier, your complexion a little duller.

Here are a few tips for this new face of yours:

* There's less light in winter. A touch more makeup brightens things up.

* From now on, it's worth taming your hair and styling it a little more than you used to.

* Your skin isn't as smooth as it once was – try not to put too much stuff on it.

* On mornings that are particularly tough, use an ice cube from the freezer on your face and under your eyes. It's an age-old remedy. Don't put the ice cube directly on your skin – wrap it in a piece of fabric and rub it gently against your face, always moving from bottom to top. Putting under-eye patches in the fridge is a plus.

COMPLEXION

* Be careful when trying to look rested. It's better to enhance your skin with foundation that seeks out the light. One trick is to mix your moisturising cream (not too heavy) with a primer.

* Prefer a glowing complexion that makes you look younger to a matte one. Choose water-based foundation, powder foundation or beauty balm, which are thin and light and will smooth out the skin, instead of oil-based foundation, which draws out imperfections.

* Opt for a cream blush, and don't go overboard with powder. Powder can settle into little wrinkles and call attention to them.

EYES

* To make your eyes stand out, add black eyeliner on the top rim of each eye.

* Go easy with overly defined kohl under the eye, it darkens your look and emphasises bags. Instead, try a gentler, more muted eye shadow.

* When putting on eyeliner, raise the line just before you reach the end of the eyelid, making a wing that lifts up instead of falling back down. Accentuate the cat eye upwards for a natural lift.

* Avoid iridescent eye shadow that can make wrinkles stand out, and opt instead for matte shades.

* Brighten the inner corner of the eye, as it tends to get darker as you get older.

* Curl your eyelashes to lift your gaze a bit.

* No skipping mascara anymore – your eyelashes aren't as plentiful as they once were.

* Beige, taupe, brown and bronze will always be very chic. For darker skin tones, try purples, blues or subtle colours that contrast with your complexion, like burgundy, cherry, maroon, chocolate and plum.

EYEBROWS

* Attend to your eyebrows hair by hair, because they're thinning out. First brush them down and draw in any sparsely populated areas; then brush them back upwards and fix them in place with a clear gel to give your eyelid an immediate lift.

* Use a chestnut or dark brown eyebrow pencil, but not black.

MOUTH

* As your lips' contours become less defined, don't overdraw them with lip pencils that will expose the fine lines around your mouth. Instead, try tracing the outline of your lips with concealer to plump them up.

* Lipstick that's too dark will only age you.

What Would
Keith Richards Do?

Diana Vreeland, the famous editor-in-chief of American *Vogue,* said time and again: 'The eye has to travel.' In the sixties, when this iconic woman was at its helm, *Vogue* paid a lot of attention to artists and intellectuals. And it wasn't just for show. Their presence makes sense on a very profound level, reflecting an essential back-and-forth between form and substance. Because inspiration never comes down to fashion alone – otherwise, we'd only ever talk about clothes, not style.

Borrowing from art, style is a way of knowing. Of accepting our own imperfections and making the best of them. It's a philosophy that always guides our steps, varying with the muses of the moment.

Style is a way of taking on the world, of breathing in its scent. We filter it through our own unique, different tastes, making it our own.

Three muses we steal from:

When we slip into a jacket we like, but whose strict cut flirts with old-lady territory, we ask ourselves one simple question: what would **Keith Richards** do? He'd probably have worn it with low-rise trousers and a half-unbuttoned shirt, showing off his chest and a tangle of necklaces with no fear of overdoing it.

Mark Rothko: What's a painter doing on this list? Rothko teaches us about colour and how the red is reinforced by the presence of its complementary colour – a strong concept when taking, for example, an overly blue outfit to the next level. Balancing it out with an accessory in the orange scale will produce interesting and original results. Let's be clear, we don't immediately think of Rothko when opening up our closets. But thanks to the time we spend in museums, among other places, some things sink in, germinate, and inspire us from afar.

Grace Jones embodies the idea that age can be liberating. That we can get away with not one but two strong fashion statements at the same time, without worrying that we're going too far. The very red lipstick + the shoulder pads or fluorescent leggings + the tomboy haircut . . . make a statement and attract attention. Do what you want, the way you want – as long as you own it.

LOVE
IS A
GAME

When you left singledom, love was something you took more or less seriously. You withdrew for the duration of a long and passionate love story that, like all long and passionate love stories, ended badly. **So here you are, back in town, thinking you'll find the world the way you left it.** You picture a short-lived, pleasant time alone, a moment to pause just long enough for you to catch your breath. You announce the news to your friends, hoping for their support and some sound advice. And sure enough, they do have some advice for you. Or, to be precise, one piece of advice – and it's always the same, no matter how they phrase it: did you download the apps? Have you made your profile yet?

Your closest friends are worried about you. Because it's assumed that a woman fresh out of a relationship has only one thing in mind: to get back into one. And this wish is difficult to implement. Your friends fill you in immediately: from now on, your love life – and/or your sex life – depends on a *game* you have to play. It's role-playing on a global scale, where people reveal themselves through the traits of an avatar that's not exactly them, but not exactly someone else either – to avoid an awkward reality check later. Now everyone meets online. What used to be a rare and anecdotal practice has become the norm throughout the world. No smartphone? No flirting. Dead battery? Sorry, no sex for you. J, an old friend who's been on the market for a few months now, laughs at your naïveté and at the aghast look on your face. Where have you been the past ten years? Well, that's easy: you were happily settled (for life, or so you thought) in a little selfish bubble, where you half-listened to other people's stories, the matches that worked out and the ones that didn't. For you, a match is tennis, a sport – not a potential love affair.

'But love is a sport.' J smiles. He seems exhausted, dark rings etched beneath his eyes. 'I'm tired but happy,' he informs you. He has a profile, of course. He works hard and packs his schedule.

He's engaged in dozens of simultaneous conversations with dozens of virtual women. It's as if he's taking care of an army of Tamagotchi pets. He has to look after them, feed them with nice words, convince each one that they're important. J admits, laughing, that sometimes he confuses them, tells the same story twice, loses some along the way. He's on the road to becoming a sexual NGO: there's a little for everyone, no matter who. He's slept with men, two women at the same time, he has fallen in love once . . . The game allows for new, exciting horizons. He extols the novelty, the experience, the appeal of letting go.

And yet you still have no desire to download the apps, to walk the walk, to sign up for this process that feels like going to an employment office for your personal life, where you're supposed to accept every opportunity that comes your way without objection. And yes, my friend, times are hard. It turns out there's a shortage of men. And no wonder, because women are supposedly all searching for stability. But the game perpetuates the game – it's the logic of the game's economy that people meet but stay single, and keep searching. In all of these organised meetings there's a feeling of programmed obsolescence. People get together for a while and then get restless, because new little Tamagotchis start screaming for attention on their screens – and they're just so cute. So one day, inevitably, they go back to the app. The game resumes, it's a vicious cycle.

But if you're perfectly honest with yourself, there are other things that keep you from joining. Since the breakup, you've been more conscious of your body. This body of yours has an age. With your ex you didn't feel the weight of the passing years – years you accumulated together and, as if in a mirror, placed you

on the same footing. Together you put on a little weight, together you developed a few wrinkles. Your relationship gave you something of a gentle truce with time, an understanding, a kind of indulgence. But now, inspecting yourself naked in the mirror, you can see only one thing: you're not twenty anymore. It's as though you'd put on corrective glasses and can now see your outline all too clearly. You look scathingly at the heaviness around your hips. The skin around your knees reminds you of wrinkled linen. And then, of course, there are those two initials tattooed right down under your belly button. Useless to try to explain those away, anyone who sees them will know immediately what they're about, reinforcing the idea that what's below is secondhand. You're afraid you'll barely know how to come anymore – you'll be so distracted by these thoughts. You delete the app J (that traitor) has surreptitiously installed on your phone.

When Mother's Day arrives, you go visit your mother in the small town where you grew up. It turns out you do want to spend time with her. She's a valuable refuge, and your separation has brought you closer. Her home has become a symbol of the world that used to be. Your father reads the newspaper (the print edition) in silence. Your mother doesn't tell him she's bored. And so it goes. This old heteronormative cliché seems almost sweet to you now. When it's time for you to leave, you realise you forgot to book a return ticket – driven most likely by a secret desire to stay longer. Of course, the trains are now all full. Your father lifts his head out of the paper and suggests you use a carpool app. You wince, thinking that even he has succumbed to the convenience of technology. Maybe it's a sign that you should give it a chance.

You find a posting that interests you. Thierry, thirty-two, is leaving from the city in an hour. He's highly rated, a safe driver, praised for his sense of humour. You create a profile, send him a request. And you wait. The minutes pass: nothing. You start to compulsively refresh the page. You get excited, you get anxious, you panic. Finally you receive a notification that Thierry has rejected your request. WTF! Did you just get blown off by a carpool?

You won't be joining Tinder anytime soon, or so you think.

YOU KNOW THINGS AREN'T
WHAT THEY USED TO BE

WHEN THE PRESIDENT OF FRANCE IS YOUNGER THAN YOU.

AN ODE TO
IMPERFECTION

Remember the popular girls in high school? The ones who were born with perfect teeth. The ones who seemed unaffected by the hormonal chaos of puberty that plagued the rest of us, who somehow lived without acne, without smelly feet and without existential angst. They could eat a chocolate croissant for breakfast, a crêpe with sugar as a snack and profiteroles for dessert without ever gaining a single pound. These were the queen bees, to whom life had decided to give all the best physical attributes, around whom boys sprouted like mushrooms in autumn – all they had to do was bend down and pick one.

But what happened to them?

It's been a few years since you stopped hearing their names . . . as if these 'it' girls have been eclipsed by the other girls – the ones you never saw coming. These other girls were less spectacular, less perfect, but they worked with what they had. Some of them even turned their flaws into a trademark. These were the girls who decided that their prominent noses had a certain sex appeal or that their uneven teeth were actually the cutest things in the world.

These imperfections, which the teenage girl hates and the woman learns to cherish, reveal a true strength of character. Our flaws give us the choice to redefine our standards of beauty – to affirm ourselves despite (and sometimes to challenge) the consensus. And we make this affirmation so boldly that we end up victorious.

We're lucky to be born with a face that we like. Or not. Fortunately, we have a lifetime to balance out injustices.

YOU KNOW THINGS AREN'T
WHAT THEY USED TO BE

WHEN YOU HAVE MORE HANGOVERS THAN ACTUAL PARTIES.

Better Butt

You've been a part of my life I could never forget,
And you've never once left my (back)side.
You've been there each step of the way – and yet
You were something I thought I should hide:

Two moons, with such mass
I could never escape you, my ass.
If I am your planet
Why is my life stuck in your orbit, goddamnit?

During the nineties,
You were told to be tiny,
So I tugged on my shirts in anguish,
Hoping I could make you vanish.

I thought you were a curse.
You wouldn't go away, no matter how I coerced.
I tried to fit you into a mould.
I starved myself to make you less bold.
I dreamed of the day you would do as you were told.

I blamed all my woes on your existence,
Without realising that I was suffering from a societal norm
From a completely unjust idea that women's bodies
Should be flattened and constrained to one-size-fits-all,
Without allowing for individuality or curves.

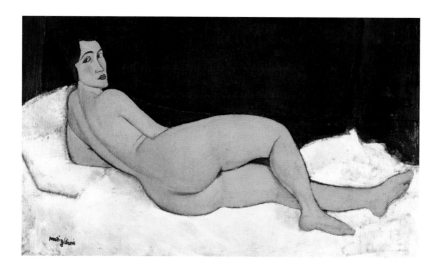

As the years passed, my thinking gradually changed
And I realised how foolish I had been
Thinking I would only be happier, if you were thin.
I shouldn't have followed what the trends decree
When they are born and die so very quickly.

With time, my complex has ripened and changed.
I now know that this butt will remain.
Never again will I hide my curves.
I'll finally give them the love they deserve.

I owe you an apology.
Don't ever leave me.
Stay round and fat.
Exactly as you are.
Cheeky.

The world may judge me,
Still, I'll say it proudly:
I love you, butt.

The Midlife Crisis

You're listening to the same song over and over again, you're thinking about a guy, you don't want to do anything serious, you reluctantly attempt to keep up the illusion of being an adult for a few hours every day – but in your head you're far, far away, and you feel like you're fifteen again.

You're in the middle of a magnificent, full-blown midlife crisis. No one warned you, or perhaps they explained it badly. For you, the word *crisis* itself conjured up something terrible and painful. A crisis was all about a medical crisis, a housing crisis, a work crisis.

You hadn't understood that this crisis could be a delicious moment, that it could feel like a holiday – that it would mean setting aside everything you'd built in order to concentrate on your own pleasure, on having heart-pounding *fun,* and on feeling vibrantly alive like you never have before.

You'd always thought that the midlife crisis was a particularly male ailment, striking primarily out-of-touch guys who can't accept that they're going bald and who frantically try to stay in the game. You never imagined it would hit you too – that you would jump on this rollercoaster thinking it might be the last time, that you would feel so light-headed, that you would throw any regrets to the wind, and that morality would, for a fleeting moment, turn a blind eye.

You look at other women, the strangers you pass on the street, wondering if many of them, like you, are carrying the same secret: this incredible feeling that nothing is ever set in stone, or at least not completely.

So you write these lines down to preserve the memory, of these contradictory emotions – a mix of joy and fear – which have the force and sophistication of a hormone-crazed teenager's diary. You're already sensing that they'll soon be a thing of the past. A crisis, in its very essence, is a passing state. Thank God.

ABOUT
PLASTIC SURGERY

In France, if you can tell someone's had a face-lift, it's considered a botched job.

It's cultural, a question of taste, it's not about passing judgement on another woman's relationship to plastic surgery. Either way, we're all curious about the subject, we want to know how the girls who took the plunge feel, we scour the Internet for before and after shots, and then we hesitate, we ponder...A thousand questions assail us.

Pros and Cons

∗ I don't want to look like a crap version of someone else. (–)

∗ **I want to look like a better version of myself. (+)**

∗ I refuse to be ashamed of my wrinkles. (–)

∗ **Why reject progress? (+)**

∗ I want to be attractive for as long as possible. (+)

∗ **I want to learn how to seduce differently. (–)**

∗ Not feeling self-conscious about my nose changed my life. (+)

∗ **Bad breast implants almost cost me my life. (–)**

∗ Why should I change because of how others see me? (–)

∗ **I'm not doing it for others, I'm doing it for myself! (+)**

∗ As long as it doesn't bother me, I'd rather wait. (–)

∗ **I want to avoid touching anything for as long as possible. (–)**

∗ The younger you start, the fewer wrinkles you'll get. (+)

∗ **I don't want to suffer any post-op side-effects. (–)**

∗ I don't want to end up looking disfigured. (–)

∗ **I don't want to look old. (+)**

∗ I want to look at myself in the mirror with pride. (+ –)

YOU KNOW THINGS AREN'T
WHAT THEY USED TO BE

When you share
an anecdote from
ten years ago and
realize it's
actually been
twenty.

I Hate

* this new double eyelid

* when people call me Madam

* watching my skin start to sag

* when I'm hanging out with a twenty-year-old and someone asks if I'm their mother

* having to put on makeup every morning

* that the cute guy didn't even look at me

* when people look at my passport

* my stray white hairs

* gaining two pounds every time I eat something delicious

* that my parents are sick

* that photo of me now that can't possibly be me

* having to behave responsibly

* getting older

THE INVISIBLE WOMAN

That mysterious girl at the party used to be me. That's really what the boys called me. Today they call me 'Madam', and usually when they need something . . . *Madam, could I bum a cigarette?* It's surprising (well, it surprised me, anyway). And yet Batman warned us this would happen: *Things change,* he said. Idiots that we are, we didn't listen.

The problem is that things change gradually, a little like the skin loosening around your chin or the effects of climate change. It takes time, a long time, to realise that the tables have turned on us.

In my case it took a few months, a few years even, for the terrible reality to sink in: **I was no longer the girl men flirted with at parties,** the one who got free drinks, who drew all eyes to her on the dance floor, who was approached nervously for her number, and who men offered to walk home.

I was becoming The Invisible Woman. The one people talk to while scanning the room behind her shoulder, left high and dry with a 'I'm going to get a drink, it was nice talking to you.'

From that point on, I had a few options:

The first was to stay home. Skip the parties, restaurants, club nights, weddings and become an antisocial killjoy who went to bed at nine. Effective, but mind-numbing.

Or I could attend only events where I was under the average age. Charity dinners, the opera, retirement parties and second or third marriages. I'd be bored out of my skull, but back to *Miss*.

I needed a third solution, one that would make me visible again, *a shift in attitude.* At parties, instead of being looked at, waiting nonchalantly at the corner of the bar for someone to ask for my number, I took the lead: I became my own propositioning force, approaching others, striking up conversation.

Sure, you have to swallow your pride and you will get blown off a few times *(Are you a friend of my mother's?).* But then you let go on the dance floor, stop checking yourself out, and enjoy the music. Become one who proposes rather than disposes, one who bursts out laughing instead of smiling stiffly. And so what if you go home alone, or if you met prettier, younger girls than you? You fall asleep with a smile, which is cheaper than a night cream and just as rejuvenating.

The Password

No one ever thinks about their Wi-Fi password. You mindlessly set it the day you move in, the computer does the remembering, and *basta,* you move on. Well, this is a mistake. There comes a day when inevitably someone will ask, 'What's the Wi-Fi password?' You'd really rather not share, because it is totally ridiculous. Anyone asking will probably read into it some deeper meaning, one they think you *intentionally* wanted to convey when you chose it: Glamour30. Ugh. As soon as it's out, you feel the need to justify. No, it's not your favourite adjective, nor how you'd describe yourself in one word, it's the name of the magazine you worked for when you moved in. And you happened to be thirty then. You are thus reminded that you once worked for a women's magazine, which seems a world away, and you haven't been thirty for a while now. Seriously, Glamour30. Sounds like a bad pop song from the nineties.

A quick survey among friends and you realise you're not the only one who made this mistake. One friend combined her last name with her ex-husband's, and it's now the only place in which

their names are still connected to this day, stuck together like a bad sex position. Nowadays they don't talk to each other. Another friend picked rocknroll, in memory of a time when music was her life. But what respectable forty-year-old woman can share rocknroll as a Wi-Fi password without looking like she can't let go of her teen years? Another one kept the original password that came with her router, a bunch of nonsensical letters and numbers that she never wrote down (and still can't find), since she thought she wouldn't stay long at that address. She's never left . . .

You start to grasp the psychological implications of this code, and just how much it says about the person who innocently created it. It marks a moment, captures it like a bad snapshot forever imprisoned in the network. You'd like to go back in time and change the lock, but you haven't got the faintest idea how. You recently read an article on computer programmers and how they think up IT systems for the masses. You've noticed a recurring term: *intuitive*. In short, these systems are set up to be used by a predominantly young section of the population who some-

how, without even thinking about it, know how to figure it out. Whereas here you are, searching in vain, clicking, cursing under your breath, trying the exact same thing ten times in a row. You press on all the buttons, still doesn't work, you get annoyed, you start talking to your computer, you even speak to it quite sharply. Fucking fuck. Nothing's working, and from now on you belong to a specific category: the *counter*intuitive. It's basically a euphemism for outdated: you and your old password. And so you resign yourself to being a thirty-year-old 'glamour girl' forever, stuck in the past.

To make matters worse, you're having lunch at your parents' tomorrow. You don't really feel like it, but you make yourself go like the good 'glamour girl' that you are – now you can't get it out of your head. Your mother sets the table while updating you on your aunts' and uncles' lives, not that you asked. When suddenly you hear a strange sound. Your mother turns around abruptly and slams her smartphone on the table. She'd told your father she didn't want this awful machine, this machine that won't stop making that unbearable noise. She'd much rather have her old mobile phone: simple, easy, just a phone, no extras. Carefully you take the object into your hands, turn off 'vibrate' and give it back to your mother. There, it's over. For a moment, you detect admiration in her eyes. You're an amazing symbol of youth, a product of modern times. You savour this feeling, this tiny victory. Sure, maybe you can't change passwords, but at least here you can pretend. And suddenly technology reconciles you with the idea of your family, in this magical world where everything goes so fast, where in a blink of an eye you're outdated.

'Nature gives you the face
you have at twenty.
It is up to you to merit the face
you have at fifty.'

*

— COCO CHANEL

YOU KNOW THINGS AREN'T
WHAT THEY USED TO BE

When you no longer know
who all the hip actors
or singers are.

Older
but
Better

You discover a photo of yourself, twenty years back. You marvel at your former body, which seems insultingly youthful. You'd forgotten how desirable it had been, so round, so firm – with all that innocence and freshness. You can't believe that you once hated this body, or how you insulted it, reproaching it constantly for not being enough *this,* too much *that,* this poor body that was never quite right, because your breasts weren't big enough, your stomach not flat enough, your thighs too shapely, your butt too flat . . . Today, you regret having been so hung up on it, for no reason, and for wasting hours moping when actually you were gorgeous. You were perfect and you had no idea. Today, after several pregnancies, not a day goes by when you don't miss the body that used to make you suffer so, noticing the wear and tear of time on your skin and muscles.

And yet . . .

Paradoxically . . .

The (truly) flawed body you have today brings you more pleasure than it ever did before.

When you reflect upon your sex life around when this photo was taken, you realise that it was far less interesting, because it was all over the place, because you didn't know yourself well enough, or because you weren't in touch with your true desires. After almost twenty years of learning, you have got to understand your real self. And now you can play your body as you would a demanding, finicky and delicate instrument – whose difficulties you've mastered, and whose chords you know by heart.

You allow yourself things you'd never dared before. You talk, you speak openly about your pleasure.

You're no longer trying to demonstrate a *savoir-faire*, you listen to your partner and above all to yourself.

You don't hesitate before asking what they're into.

You don't watch yourself, you seek their pleasure and your own. Sometimes you only find your own and you accept this necessary selfishness. You couldn't care less about hearing you're good in bed, because everyone's been good or bad with someone. What matters is that you're there, really there every time. You're not trying to reenact some porn video but to find and give pleasure.

Your sex life is now more inspired, passionate and free than it was in the days of that perfect body. For once, older really is better.

YOU KNOW THINGS AREN'T
WHAT THEY USED TO BE

WHEN YOU GO TO
THE OB-GYN FOR
MAMMOGRAMS RATHER
THAN BIRTH CONTROL.

THE NEEDLE
AS A WEAPON

You'd like to give a shout-out to science, doctors and everyone else who contributed to this essential step forward for humankind. You think we should publicly recognise the importance of plastic surgery in the fight for gender equality. No, you're not joking. You are convinced that the needle is at heart a political weapon. That Botox corrects more than just wrinkles – it corrects basic biological injustice. Here's why.

You were raised to believe that we should fight to establish equality between men and women. You've been even more convinced of this ever since you read that damn article on male and female hormones. You discovered that andropause had recently been renamed LOH, or late-onset hypogonadism. Why? Because as men age, their male hormones diminish, but their bodies never entirely stop producing them. Whereas female hormones eventually disappear for good, total breakdown, like a wheel that rolls for a while and then finally tips onto one side. **Conclusion: Mother Nature is a bitch, and probably a misogynist.** She didn't bother looking out for her own kind. And the war against the passing of time isn't fought, naturally, with equal weapons.

Also, you think that every woman who's felt the need (and has the option . . .) to get plastic surgery has every right to do so as she desires. She has the right to fix her wrinkles and the biological deficits her body is undergoing. She has the right to grab hold of time, after everything it's put her through, and twist it however she likes. A way to reset the dial to zero, so to speak. To fight back against the expression that is sexist and violent: an old cow, which the French literally refer to as an 'old skin'. You like that human intelligence has found a solution for this original sin against our bodies. What's important with surgery isn't getting it, but having the choice.

All Those Times You Tell Yourself You're Exercising

(When Actually You're Not)

When you flex your butt while brushing your teeth.

When you flex your butt again while waiting for the lift.

When you finally decide to take the stairs.

When you make love. You read in some magazine about the quantitative relationship between sex and energy expenditure. The 150 calories on average, per go, really adds up.

When you carry your child in one arm, and change sides regularly, he's basically a dumbbell.

When you dance (while drinking) and you persuade yourself that sweating is proof of your muscular exertion (and not just a sign that your body is trying to get rid of the alcohol through the pores of your skin).

When you leave late for a meeting and you walk very fast to try to get there on time, you tell yourself that there are speed-walking competitions, so you are working out.

When you make risotto and stir the saucepan with regular motions for two hours, standing upright.

When you rode your bike to work, until your bike got stolen. It was a good month while it lasted.

When you watch football on TV, shouting in support of your team, and you end up exhausted, concluding, 'WE played well.'

When you sit in a sauna. Because you have decided that this qualifies as 'exercise'.

When you hold in your pee for a really long time.

When you try to remember something, because your memory is a muscle too.

When
It Sucks

Y ou didn't expect to run into her, not tonight, not like this. You dated this girl a while ago, for a few weeks, maybe a few months. You have good memories of her . . . a little hazy . . . but pleasant. And here she is, coming towards you to say hello, smiling. But you're freaking out. You want to disappear, to be swallowed into the floor. Why? Because you can't remember her damn name. Juliette? Gabriella? It's not that there have been so many lovers in your life you've forgotten, oh, no. You just can't remember because . . . it was a VERY long time ago! You feel embarrassed, you cringe. These are moments that you've buried deep inside yourself, that you haven't confessed to anyone and weren't really proud of . . .

Some other moments when it sucks:

That time someone asks your age and innocently you shave off a year. The worst is you didn't even try to lie – it simply hasn't sunk in yet that you're a year older now.

The day you realise the reason you're so annoyed by this girl at work – the one everyone else finds so charming and that you find utterly dull and pretentious – is quite simply because you're jealous of her. Because, truly, her single and essential flaw is that she is much younger than you.

When your hairdresser recommends a cut by saying it will make you look younger, or when the waitress calls you Madam and you reassure yourself she's doing it on purpose just to annoy you.

When you find a woman your age looking a lot older than you do . . . and are secretly thrilled that you're better preserved. (And what you don't know is she's thinking the exact same thing about you.)

So we're all in the same boat with that girl inside us who's not quite the beautiful person we all dream ourselves to be. A fault confessed is half redressed, right?

YOU KNOW THINGS AREN'T
WHAT THEY USED TO BE

When you're excited
just to go home.

ooking around your little flat this morning – and out the window at the neighbours across the way with whom you share a not-entirely-consenting proximity – you feel a twinge of claustrophobia. The next minute you're thinking about the exorbitant price that you pay for this dark second-floor studio, so you come to the conclusion that **something clearly isn't right and needs to change.**

Without going all the way back to Darwin, as a human being in touch with your animal side, you know you came from nature and you need nature. And that amid the greyness of this concrete jungle, you could find a similar flat near a park this time, to quench your vital need for chlorophyll – a need that previously, let's face it, you'd been in touch with only through the mint in your mojito.

You decide to check out the property ads (what's to lose?). If you were lucky enough to find a place with a clear view and sunlight filtering through some leaves, imagine the impact on your quality of life. Alas, a few listings in, you quickly hit a snag: for the same square footage you currently have, prices have gone through the roof . . . as if for every urban dweller, getting a bit closer to a tree trunk has the same effect on prices as having a room with a view in a five-star hotel.

Dreaming
Green

What if, just out of curiosity, you looked a bit farther afield, just outside of the city . . . in the countryside. Why do things half-way? A few years ago, no amount of money would have got you to leave, but that was then . . . before you stopped smoking, before you considered joining your friend at her yoga class, before you decided to take care of yourself – healthy body, healthy mind – with the fervour of a religious convert.

To your great surprise, you end up finding what you're looking for: a pretty little house, affordable, three times the size of your current studio, with a spare room, calm and with a garden too – just calling out to you. What are you waiting for? This is just what you need! Think of those breakfasts you'd have outside, the dog you could adopt, the walks in the forest, mushroom picking in the autumn, living by the rhythm of the seasons, and when you got back in the evening, you'd light a fire. You could even plant flowers, start a vegetable garden, eat what you grow – real organic produce, not like the stuff you overpay for now, without even knowing where it really comes from. You could be living that dream.

Okay, sure, you'd need to take the train, wake up a little earlier – but doesn't the early bird get the worm? You could leave your bike at the station and ride to your office – nothing better than a little exercise. Your complexion would be rosy, your legs firm, your bio-rhythm boosted and your red blood cell levels would match those of a ten-year-old. Green with envy of your new life and body, your friends would start searching for their own little Eden, joining the movement.

But what about deciding to go to a party or a movie on the spur of the moment; the art shows, your little neighbourhood restaurant, the twenty-four-hour deli, so convenient for late-night cravings? And what about booty calls? What would happen to spontaneity, what will become of all that?

You don't accept defeat. With your eye on the prize, you head down to the florist and come bounding back up the stairs with three little potted plants to set on your windowsill: basil, mint and cherry tomato. You've never had a green thumb, but you have to start somewhere.

Things You Told Yourself You'd Never Say, Part I

Are you sure we're the same age? She seems so much older.

Back in my day, things didn't just fall into your lap.

When I was little, the Internet didn't exist.

Don't you think the music is a bit loud?

You know it's good to be bored sometimes, it stimulates the imagination.

Ask your father.

Sit up properly in your chair.

Shut up – she could be his daughter!

How did we survive without mobile phones? Just fine, actually.

And to think that I knew you when you were tiny.

Santa Claus won't be happy . . .

Okay, she's cute now, but just give her ten years...

How are you kids?

I just can't go out two nights in a row anymore.

Give me a break, I was your age once too.

That was trendy when I was a teenager.

I wonder if I need reading glasses.

In my day, we invented games all the time.

I'm happy to go out, but I need to be in bed by midnight.

I can't take alcohol anymore, if I drink it takes me two days to recover.

Do you have SPF 50?

YOU KNOW THINGS AREN'T
WHAT THEY USED TO BE

WHEN YOU WAKE UP FEELING GREAT AND EVERYONE TELLS YOU HOW TIRED YOU LOOK.

WERE
YOUR
TWENTIES
THE
BEST
YEARS?

n his 1938 novel *The Conspiracy,* Paul Nizan writes: '**I was twenty once, and I won't let anyone say those are the best years of your life.**' This sentence, quite famous in France, always made me feel less lonely. My twenties weren't the best time either. I spent them thinking they should be extraordinary, exciting and romantic, and I couldn't make it happen. Nothing happened at all, in fact, and it was terribly distressing. That decade felt so heavy when it should have been carefree.

Oh, how serious I was at twenty . . . I was paralysed by opportunities I wasn't taking, but how could I take risks in a world already so chaotic? I was afraid of dying before I'd truly lived, but too careful to live at all. I was scared of not becoming somebody and had no clue which somebody to be. Instead of being me, I got trapped in false identities of my own making.

I thought that every decision would be monumental and fateful, engraved in stone forever. I thought I should succeed before I'd even started on my journey. I believed this with such conviction that it suffocated me. Any direction I went would be misguided, I felt like I was standing on the platform with everyone around me boarding their trains, I didn't have the right instruction manual, I wasn't born in the right place at the right time, I didn't have what it takes to make it, my choices would corner me forever like a marriage I could never get out of.

I had so many fears back then that today I'm not afraid. ✳ **I know that if I don't reach for it, no one will give it to me. Sometimes all you need is to give yourself permission.** ✳ I know that I will never regret my misadventures. ✳ **And that sometimes failures are successes in disguise.** ✳ I know that you can take the wrong path and it's okay. ✳ **That we must be grateful for what we have.** ✳ I know to take life one day at a time. That life is what we make of every day. ✳ **I know not to cry over lost loves, because we fall in love again and again.** ✳ I know how to love and be loved. ✳ **I know that sometimes you have to shake things up to avoid repeating the same mistakes.** ✳ And that smiling is one of life's greatest weapons. ✳ **I know that something better is always on its way.** ✳ And that there's always a light after the storm. ✳ **I know that you can't work hard if you don't have fun, and that you can't have fun if you don't work hard.** ✳ I know that if you give, you will receive. ✳ **I know not to force it if stuck, but choose another path instead.** ✳ Nothing is forever. ✳ **I know that working out gives you a healthy mind.** ✳ I'm happier now than I was at twenty, and no one ever warned me back then. ✳

'One is not born,

but rather becomes,

a woman.'

*

—SIMONE DE BEAUVOIR,

THE SECOND SEX

How Old Are You?

s our age the one that's inked in our ID? Not necessarily . . . When staring at the mirror in despair, thinking,
'I'm eighteen, trapped in the body of a woman twice my
age,' age becomes a relative notion. Think of the child who's an
old soul, or the twinkle in the eye of a centenarian. There's proof
enough around us that age alone is insufficient, and vague. It
tells us nothing specific beyond its administrative function.

Age is particular, and disconcerting. The age we feel is in our soul
and in our heart, not just a number that ticks upwards at every
birthday like the odometer of a car.

A woman feels, on average, seven to ten years younger than what
her birth certificate betrays. So they say, and it depends on the
person. But it also depends on the moment, we might add – and
over the course of one day we might feel like an old woman in the
morning and a teen at night.

**So here we are with many different ages: an age of birth,
and an emotional age.** An age imposed by nature, and one
we can determine for ourselves. That painful question of 'How
old are you?' can thus outwit the fatalism of the answer it com-
mands. Age becomes a costume we change into, a mood that we
can dissipate.

That's why we might feel equal to people of all ages, why friendships grow across different generations. You're not the same age as your arteries. You are the age of your desires, of your passions and your interests.

The Truth,
the Whole Truth,
and Nothing
but the Truth

'He couldn't believe it when he realised she was my little sister.'
(= *Please tell me she looks older than me.*)

'I only smoke at parties.'
(= *I smoke much more than that, but I sneak the rest of them.*)

'I'm allergic to gluten, it's horrible, I can't eat a thing.'
(= *I have a complicated relationship with my weight.*)

'Did you know people keep saying I have a thing with Paul?'
(= *Do you think I have a chance with Paul?*)

'I'm worried, my son's teacher says he's precocious.'
(= *I always knew he was a genius.*)

'I usually never drink at lunchtime.'
(= *I drink at lunchtime more and more often.*)

'Yes, the book really moved me, especially the beginning.'
(= *I only read the title. I don't read anymore, I just watch TV series.*)

'I've been working out a lot recently.'
(= *I'm not getting laid these days.*)

'That guy's really not great, plus he's so pretentious.'
(= *This bastard didn't even look at me.*)

'I'm an environmentalist.'
(= *I just started recycling and I turn off the tap when I brush my teeth.*)

'I'm PMSing.'
(= *I'm a bitch, get over it.*)

FAMILY
HOLIDAYS

Every year your family gathers for a weeklong holiday. There's no avoiding it, or you'd be burning bridges with your mother, father, brothers and sisters and their plus-ones – forever. You're excited at the thought of spending time in your childhood house, which holds a special place in your heart. But you also know – and the lump in your throat knows and your boyfriend also knows – that **this place is where you are 'your worst self'.**

Every year for seven days you get sucked into a vortex that you can't escape. You're right back where you started, the exact day you packed your bags and left to live your life. You were eighteen and slammed the door on your way out. Since that day, they can't see you differently and you can't see that they too have evolved. To them, you're still that eighteen-year-old girl. Take your older sister, always the clumsy one: she'll spend a week breaking all the glasses in the house, which never happens at any other time of the year. That's how it goes, we become the person others think we are and slip into old roles.

And as for you, you've been working on yourself for a long time now, juggling therapy and EMDR sessions so you can manage your traumas and neuroses, meditating often and making kindness a priority in life. It all just disappears the second you walk

through that door. You become that monster, twisting every word you hear into a personal attack. You know full well your mother guilt-trips you because she herself is filled with guilt, and at the end of the day, she's just doing her best. And then your sister, who always loved animals more than people . . . You know this nth debate is just so that you'll give her some attention.

Your tolerance is at zero and everything infuriates you. You sneak out to the back garden late at night to smoke that cigarette you got off your niece, trying to prove that you, at least, haven't turned into an old bitch. You are a forty-year-old teenage rebel.

Year after year you leave this place vowing to grow up, change for the better, become tolerant, gentle, understanding, or at least fair, and reach a level of wisdom where everyone's opinions wash right over you. Because you love these people and it pains you to hurt them – and in the process you hurt yourself too.

That Ex

You loved each other more than you could ever say. He knew you better than anyone. You went through everything together. He was under your skin, he was yours, you were his.

Yet you never made a life together. And yet you were still in love when you broke up.

'
No matter where I go, go
I will always see your face'
—LOVE

He was your first love, and you weren't ready. You were too young.

Or maybe you had a child together, but despite tremendous happiness, it didn't work out.

Or he stormed through your life like a shooting star – breaking in, then moving on in the same breath, wrecking everything in his wake.

He's the only one you refer to as 'my ex', though there were others before and after.

∗ ∗ ∗

After the breakup you felt adrift, certain you would never get another chance at this.

What would become of those embraces? There had been whispers, promises and vows. What of the smiles and the laughter, the way he'd touch you, watch you from afar, or warm your feet by entangling them with his own. Are they leftover ashes from a fire, a simple fading scar, a case closed? Or are these images and scents that you keep for your archive, and he recycles with another?

You hate that you couldn't shake the feeling, that he got to decide it was over, when the connection between you was so strong. Your friends responded with that unbearable cliché: 'Love alone isn't enough . . .' They advised you to move on, get drunk and mix with other bodies and trust the age-old rule: new skin will fill the void. But that didn't work – all it did was reinforce his absence. At the urging of your loved ones, you finally deleted the songs you listened to together from your phone. You even gave the clothes he left behind to people who wouldn't know their history. On the surface things were getting better, but he was monopolising the secret, intimate part of your life. **You still had conversations with him in your mind.** Days, weeks, months passed, and you still battled with bare hands this now imaginary being who invaded you. How much time, patience and perseverance would it take for him to finally get the hell out? Desperate times call for desperate measures: You moved to avoid walking past the place where you kissed for the last time. A change of scene for a change of mind.

Time does heal wounds. You have finally tamed that feeling of loss and absence. Now you smile at the memories you stumble across: letters you wrote to him, photographs, hearing your song in a taxi.

And when you happen to run into him, you blush and even sweat a little, embarrassment tinged with the emotion of seeing him again – but you know the score. Sure, you'd reconnect, fall back into your old habits and complicity, but inevitably a very precise moment would come when you would remember why you're no longer together.

In *Mad Love,* André Breton says, 'I was lost, you came to give me news of myself.' So you started wondering: Why him? And, above all, **why did it take so long before you allowed yourself to love again?** By holding on to this past love, weren't you protecting your convictions and a part of yourself that you didn't want to let die? Maybe this ex was exactly who you needed *at the time,* like the process of developing a photo, an act of learning: to reveal yourself. Not before, not after. And therefore not necessarily for life.

Now you're not even sure you would fall in love with him had you not known him from before. It doesn't really matter. Deep down, your fondness and affection are intact, hidden away, in a place belonging only to the two of you, and it takes nothing away from the loves who have followed.

> 'No matter where you go, go
> You will always see my face'
> —LOVE

Wrinkles

Sunshine gives you wrinkles.

Smiling gives you wrinkles.

Partying gives you wrinkles.

My god, how dull life must be for people with no wrinkles.

Crazy Absurd Recipes

Throughout the ages, queens, princesses and smooth-talking peddlers have looked for tricks to keep us looking young and fresh-faced. These secrets to staying beautiful have been inscribed in grimoires and memoirs we can still reference today. Note how absurd and irrational these beliefs were. Some were downright poisonous! Which leads us to question our own routines. What will future generations think of our golden masks and our silk-fibre shampoo? Will they be as horrified as we are by those before us? Will they think that we were batshit crazy to believe that a collagen mask could smooth out the wrinkles on our eyelids? Here's a short anthology of our ancestors' wildest and wackiest cosmetic habits.

Forehead Waxing: In the Middle Ages, the forehead was the pinnacle of beauty, and the bigger the better. It had to be perfectly smooth, as round as possible, like a little ball of dough. What we would find about as sexy as E.T. was considered the height of fashion. Women would wax their forehead, some going so far as

to shave the front of their head to push back their hairline. For the waxing, they prepared a sort of 'waxy' concoction of quicklime, arsenic and . . . bat's blood.

Blonde Dye: During the Renaissance, French fashion was all about 'Venetian blonde', between blonde and red hair colour. They would smear a mixture of lemon juice and saffron powder onto their hair and then sit in the sun for as long as possible, so the dye could really sink in.

Gold Dust: In the sixteenth century, Diane of Poitiers was French king Henri II's favourite, even though she was twenty years his senior. Considered in her youth to be the fairest woman in the land, she was obsessed with the idea of staying forever young. Every morning she drank a special broth, whose secret ingredient was gold dust. The elixir of youth was no doubt fatal: while trying to preserve her youth, she quite simply poisoned herself. Toxicological reports based on a lock of her hair showed a five-hundred-times-higher gold concentration than the normal level.

The Rule of Threes: Diane of Poitiers created a rule of sorts to explain what women's pillars of beauty should be. All of them revolved around the number three. For a woman to be truly beautiful, she needed for three parts of her to be white (skin, teeth, hands), three black (eyes, eyebrows, eyelids), three red (lips, cheeks, nails), three long (body, hair, fingers), three short (teeth, ears, feet), three small (nipples, nose, head), three narrow (her mouth, waistline, feet) and three large (her arms, thighs and calves).

Flawless Skin: In the eighteenth century, the little age spots that appeared on the skin were called 'lentils'. The women of the time had a solution for this that should definitely not be replicated. At night, they would coat their hands and faces with a liquor compress made from crushed viper steeped in milk, with a dash of . . . vitriolic acid! It's a mystery how their skin survived.

The Paleness of Marie Antoinette: In the eighteenth century, during Louis XVI's reign, at the court of Versailles, women underwent actual physical torture to meet the aesthetic canons of the time. The first criteron was the whiteness of their skin – to distinguish themselves, of course, from the poor peasants who slaved all day in fields under the hot sun. It was said that a woman's neck should be so white that you could 'see the wine going down her throat as she drinks'. Women would do anything to achieve such a result – even burning their skin with mercury-based cream! Marie Antoinette, with the help of her own personal parfumier, Jean-Louis Fargeon, concocted an *eau fraîche*. It required two chopped pigeons, mixed with a dozen egg whites and ground-up peach pits. It was then steeped in goat's milk for twelve hours, left out in the sun for three days and then kept in the cellar for fifteen days.

Nostradamus's Mad Mixture: Michel de Nostredame was a French apothecary known for his predictions in the sixteenth century. He also developed recipes for women to use, inventing a cream to make a fifty-five-year-old woman look . . . twelve! It required mixing sublimated mercury (downright toxic) with the saliva from someone who had ingested nothing but garlic for three days

(holy halitosis). Using a marble mortar and pestle, this then got blended with vinegar and powdered silver. A recipe for disaster.

Gabrielle d'Estrées's Liqueur of the Day: In the sixteenth century, Henri IV's mistress had a secret to keep her skin shimmering with beauty. She would stuff the belly of a swallow (unplucked and ungutted) with fleur-de-lis, two fresh eggs, honey, Venice turpentine, ground-up pearls and camphor. Once the swallow was cooked in a cauldron, it was crushed into a sort of cream and mixed in with musk and ambergris. It was then all distilled into a liqueur that was said to make your skin soft and firm!

THIS IS
THE LAST TIME

(Things You Won't Do Anymore, Probably)

A s you take out old photos and cringe at your post-teenage years, you remember full well that at the time you thought you'd finally found the look, the guy and the hairstyle that was meant for you.

With fondness and a tinge of nostalgia, today you look back at all you've said goodbye to:

The crazy haircuts and bad dye jobs: when you used to go to your hairdresser instead of your shrink, saying, 'I want a complete change, you have carte blanche.' Admittedly, the pixie cut and the ensuing times you were mistaken for a young man did leave a few scars. Those burgundy-auburn highlights were meant to give you a bit of sexy spunk, not a sickly look. Leave well enough alone.

Those painful purchases: that pair of jeans you bought to wear after a diet; they gave you a great silhouette but also a yeast infection. Those shoes one size too small but on sale. That pistachio-green sweater you bought just because you didn't dare tell the saleswoman you weren't sure. They all stayed in the wardrobe – or, worse, ruined an evening out or two. You don't always need to suffer to be beautiful.

Those awful pimples you'd pop mercilessly, hoping they'd disappear faster. These days, you clean them, then let time do its thing. Nature has her way.

Procrastination. Nowadays it's crystal clear: miracles are rare and you'd rather give yourself a kick in the butt than wait for a situation to get worse. Eventually.

Your inseparable friendships: you did everything together, called each other all the time, spent hours on the phone. Until it got too intrusive and you needed your own space. Now you value quality over quantity.

Those impossible, complicated, oh-so-tortured love stories: hoping that those guys who said, 'I can't be in a relationship right now, but call me if you want to hook up!' would change their minds. You now know you prefer the sweetness of a long-term relationship to the sterility of no-strings-attached one-night stands.

And finally, how often you used to say 'never'. Because you never really know. Life is full of surprises; hell, you might even surprise yourself.

REDEFINING THE RELATIONSHIP

Since your early childhood, you were told that a couple was always a man and a woman, and that they'd be together forever. Marriage and fidelity included. Your grandparents set the tone: married at twenty and until 'death do them part'. For life, then, for better and for worse. Your parents' arguing opened a new chapter in your understanding of the construct – until they got divorced, and the tension at home was replaced by relief. So you ended up with a shaky view of it all: should you believe in it, and, more important, was it still *possible*?

And what about good old monogamy? One person there with you through every stage of life, evolving at your side? A comforting theory, but in practice not so simple. After the sexual revolution of the seventies, the introduction of birth control and the frenzy of divorce as an almost anarchic freedom, **would you tear it all down and change everything, or instead take refuge in more conservative values?**

In retrospect, your love life hasn't exactly been a straight line. It wasn't what you expected or like anyone predicted. It wasn't always fun, but you've experimented, hesitated and made mistakes so as to better understand yourself. Through the good and the bad, you did things your way.

There were the transitory companions, and partners you loved passionately while knowing you could never live with them. You raised other people's kids until you met someone with whom to have your own. You fell madly in love with a woman. They all watched you grow, encouraged you, and loved in their own way. And you realised that time, longevity, the commitments it entails, isn't everything. These different kinds of love were a spectrum, never the same twice, but never wholly unique either.

In short, while the official definition of a relationship once comforted you, **your experience has shown you that you contradict yourself and are constantly changing. That you've had several lives.**
What will the next one be, and ideally, will you build it to last?

As if for guidance, you start observing your friends' relationships more closely and how they get by (alone, as a couple, or sometimes more). In addition to traditional relationships, you see new arrangements hatching. For example, a couple might be together but living apart. Better to have two studios than one big flat, and a relationship that lasts. You also inquire into their experience with solitude and routine, with daily life. Some openly admit not needing sex anymore. Others affirm their lack of desire to have children: they're happy with the balance in their single life or their relationship, and the responsibility of caring for someone else would threaten that harmony. As for fidelity, many tell you that they believe in it and they adhere to it (that reassures you), but also that there's value in keeping some of that intimacy a mystery. And that it's possible and even common to love someone, to fall out of love, and then to fall back in love with them again. Others have their own particular way of cheating boredom: for some it's actually cheating – for others, it's fighting temptation. Out of all that, you hold on to the advice of the wise Ruth Bader Ginsburg, 'it helps sometimes to be a little deaf', since, in the end, most of your partner's imperfections are unimportant . . . or not worth splitting up over.

At this stage in life, as new romantic opportunities present themselves, you realise some things have changed over the years. You used to want the thrill of love above all else, even if that meant suffering, exhaustion, frustration. It wasn't just the love of being in love but also probably an attempt to conform to preconceived – and not always accurate – notions of what you thought a love story should be.

Never mind the changes in society and in others – what has changed in you? Your heart, just like when you were twenty, still wants to beat wildly. But you've learned to take people as they come, whereas previously you might have been put off by their flaws, dismissing them summarily if they weren't exactly what you wanted. **You no longer demand perfection because you've learned that we're all fallible.**

'Old age is no place

for sissies.'

*

—BETTE DAVIS

Room
to
Breathe

Y ou can't pinpoint the first time someone said to you, *You have a small waist, it's lovely.* You had scarcely hit puberty and were worried about your ears growing faster than the rest of your face, and you thought your thighs were filling out your jeans too much. You were becoming aware of the growing differences between certain canons of beauty and the girl looking back at you in the mirror. **The world was shoving unrealistic beauty standards down your throat, and you swallowed them.** You didn't know any better. So when you heard: *you have a small waist,* you started to feel like the world had blessed you with a gift. Obviously you didn't hope to tick off the winning numbers – 36-24-36 – that every woman knows despite herself. But nevertheless, you seemed to have one of the numbers right, which was something.

So you were determined to look after your waist. And in time you learned to show it off. That's the short way of saying you buckled your belts so tightly that you could hardly breathe. Your body was split in two, as if the southern half of you was trying to secede from the north. You were permanently on the verge of apoplexy. Oh, sure, a small waist is beautiful, it gives you an allure . . . but you are out of breath. You learned to live in a state of torture. Both tormentor and victim at once. You went on with life – smiling, talking, walking – as if you weren't about to faint. You once found a contraption at a thrift shop that gave you the kind of silhouette to rival both Jessica Rabbit and Dita Von Teese. You could have sworn that you were walking around with a permanent Snapchat filter. Only when you took it off at night you had traces of its stitching, a bright red mark across the skin just above your hips that lingered until the following morning.

You had so thoroughly embraced the idea that one must suffer to be beautiful that you barely noticed anymore. Pain was one of your accessories. When people ask, 'What's your beauty secret?' nobody responds: 'Oh, it's simple. I just put myself through hell.' But it's true. You did it so many times. Your skirt was too tight, so you stopped eating. Your clothes need to be the right size for your body, not the other way around. You sometimes suffocated yourself just for the pleasure of wearing a turtleneck unfit for the season. Not to mention the thongs that sliced you like razors. From a purely biological point of view, it's likely that a woman takes several years off her life by dressing badly.

When you think about it, you feel stupid for having accepted the discomfort for all these years. There are so many areas in your life where you fight for gender equality, but it's a battle that stops at the door to your wardrobe. So it's with an almost militant impulse that you decide to treat yourself better. At an age when women are told they must do even more to look good, you choose to be kinder to yourself. You will loosen your belt. Don't get me wrong: you're not letting yourself go, you're not abdicating. You've decided it's time to feel better in order to look good. And you have the right, damn it. From now on, you will have room to breathe.

YOU KNOW THINGS AREN'T
WHAT THEY USED TO BE

When selecting your
year of birth
on a website means
scrolling down
forever.

Another One for the Road?

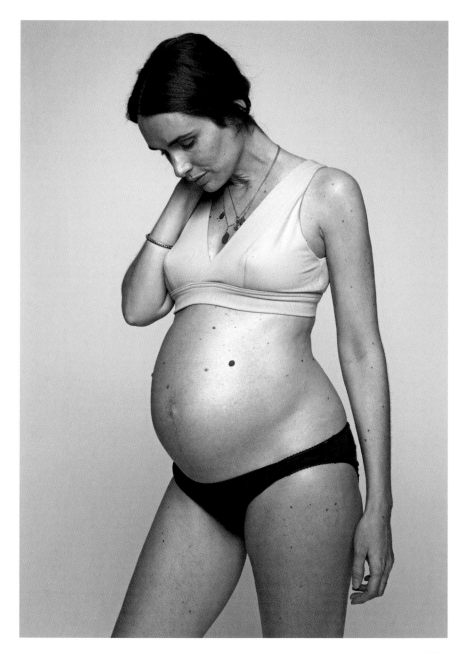

For a while now, you've had these questions on your mind:

Should the family grow?

Do I have the time? The energy?

Would our relationship survive?

Do I even have it in me to love another one?

Can I do it all – keep my job and take care of another child?

But suddenly, upon seeing a tiny baby, you tell yourself that newborns are real rascals. With their cute little faces, adorable delicate hands, and their skin that smells so sweet – not to mention the soft little hairs that stick together on their necks. Inevitably, in front of so much cuteness, you soften, you feel yourself melting . . . Then you spend the rest of the day weighing the pros and cons:

1. You know how to do this. (+)

2. The planet is already overpopulated. (–)

3. If you wait, it'll be too late to regret. (+)

4. As it is, you're struggling to make ends meet. (–)

5. Because you can't get pregnant. (–)

6. Because you want to. (+)

7. The first is a revolution, the second is an event, and the third will raise itself. (+)

8. Last time, it took you two years to lose that weight. (–)

9. The divorce rate after a second child. (–)

10. Large families are fun. (+)

11. You're finally done with nappies. (–)

12. You said 'never again' after giving birth the last time. (–)

13. Because at some point you have to stop. (–)

14. Because it would be madness! (+–)

THE TRACKS YOU STILL LISTEN TO

(And Give Away that You Were a Teen in the Nineties)

* Run DMC, 'It's Tricky'

* Nirvana, 'Heart-Shaped Box'

* Radiohead, 'Climbing Up the Walls'

* Fugees, 'Killing Me Softly'

* The Verve, 'Bitter Sweet Symphony'

* Red Hot Chili Peppers, 'Otherside'

* Fool's Garden, 'Lemon Tree'

* Coolio, 'Gangsta's Paradise'

* Rage Against the Machine, 'Killing in the Name'

* Oasis, 'Don't Look Back in Anger'

* The Offspring, 'Come Out and Play'

* Guns N' Roses, 'Don't Cry'

* Blur, 'Song 2'

* Sugar Ray, 'Hold Your Eyes'

Two lovers meet in a restaurant. They were madly in love when young – but then life happened and they parted ways. Years have gone by, and they're very happy to see each other again for dinner, in a nice neighbourhood, a restaurant where they used to hang out. The passage of time is etched in each other's faces, but they don't care. They're looking at each other through the same eyes they did back then, because the pleasure of seeing each other is still there, intact, as if it were yesterday. Sitting across from each other, they look at the menu. At that moment, the waiter arrives.

'And what would you like to order this evening?'

'Today's special,' says the woman.

'Good idea, I'll have the same,' says the man.

'Very good,' says the waiter, 'but which one?'

The man and the woman look at each other and burst out laughing . . . and each take out their glasses so they can read the menu.

It Happens
to Everyone

If you've struggled to read the story on the previous page, it's normal. That's what it feels like to need 'reading glasses' before you actually know you need them. It's a very unpleasant moment, trying on a friend's glasses only to realise that . . . life is better with them on.

Here's the thing: we don't wake up one morning with a sudden wish for spectacles. It takes years of denial before reaching that point. Here are the surefire signs that, yep, it's time, you're presbyopic.

- Weirdly, you don't enjoy reading as much as you once did.

- You can't deny the migraines threaten more and more frequently, at night, as you tuck into a good book.

- When you get the bill in restaurants, you tend to hold your arm out to bring the numbers into focus.

- You zoom in to 125 per cent when reading texts on the computer (you know what we're talking about).

Presbyopia is not an illness, just the inevitable decrease of crystallin that began at birth. It's the world's first visual defect and almost everyone goes through it . . . The good news is, a good pair of glasses can be as sexy as a good pair of legs.

A
GOOD
RUN

He smelled like sweat and cologne
You were looking at his delicate neck
He seemed very young
You liked his self-assured laugh
This laugh, when you asked him
Whose song this was
Because you were still calling it a song
You had never heard that electro track
Which his favourite station was playing
Apparently everyone knew it
He smirked – half tender, half mischievous
He hummed the lyrics
And one thing led to another
He let his guard down
He wasn't from around here
Sometimes, felt lonely
In this cutthroat city
Music was a refuge
You were watching his agile hands
Those hands without veins
Tap in rhythm to the refrain
He seemed slightly fragile, suddenly
He began to dance to amuse you

Just bobbing his shoulders and head
You surprised yourself by doing the same
And you laughed together
He promised he'd send you
The name of the famous song
Meeting his eyes in the mirror
The words came out on their own
You told him that you'd listen to it
. . . always thinking of him.
You saw his eyes scan over you
He seemed unpleasantly surprised
As if he hadn't understood
The car stopped
He barely turned around
And said: have a good day, Madam.
During those ten minutes in a car service
The time of one ride
A ride through time
You had changed age
For a fleeting moment.
You stepped onto the pavement
And seconds later,
The car left.

YOU KNOW THINGS AREN'T
WHAT THEY USED TO BE

When you start
finding biographies
fascinating.

A
New
Love

Râncuşi's famous statue *The Kiss* (*Le Baiser*) was carved from a single block of stone. Two lovers are entwined as one. This captures everything. It says it all. The eternity of love drawing strength from a tender kiss, the two lovers embracing each other to perfection, becoming one . . .

But sometimes lovers go back to being two. They separate. It's terribly painful.

And then one day, you brace yourself to kiss someone else. This moment is overwhelming, as it is nothing like you expected. You were imagining a sublime, smooth and incredibly exciting embrace – but instead you're totally destabilised. The first sensation is the most disconcerting, no doubt: you rub your skin against unknown skin, a new scent, a softness you're not familiar with . . . The other person's tongue surprises you, it's so different from the tongue you used to know. **There's something very startling about feeling a new body against your own.**

You had thought that you were ready. To be honest, you had so longed for it, so fantasised about it, that difference, that otherness. But you suddenly realise how you and your previous partner had moulded and shaped each other over time – like two stones rubbing up against each other for so long that they interlock, perfectly smooth. You told yourself that you were going to feel twenty again, all fired up with passion. But instead you're living the worst of being twenty.

The things you thought were behind you. All the fears, anxieties and unanswered questions. So maybe you should give yourself the same advice you would give to a young woman for whom it's the first time:

It's not a performance. Do only what you want to do, what you feel. Reassure your partner, who may be just as scared as you. Do nothing that feels embarrassing your first time. You have plenty of time to get to know each other, time to explore. You're not there to win a gymnastics competition. Don't get distracted by the details of your body; they don't matter to your partner in the least. What matters is the feeling in the moment.

In this new embrace, you'll become one again with someone else: your new lover, just as Brâncuşi's sculpture alluded to the early cubism and shaped a new art form.

There's something very startling about feeling a new body against your own.

STYLING TRICKS

Don't hesitate to choose a jacket or coat two sizes up.
The sharp lines will give you a more interesting allure.

A suit does not have to be navy or black for you to be taken seriously. On the contrary, this old pink brings out your determination and originality.

In the evening, swap a coat for a cape, which adds mystery
and leaves room for the unexpected.

Learn to identify those items that suit you.
They'll come in handy on bad days.

A fun accessory on a simple silhouette
always works well.

Balance out one strong item with a monochrome set – of a colour
from the strong piece itself. It will enhance it, with elegance.

Mix and unmatch your suit. It's surprising and chic . . .
And there's your new wardrobe!

HOW
DAVID BOWIE
SAVED
YOUR LIFE

January 10 2016.

You are shaking. David Bowie is dead. You could pretend it's the melomaniac inside you tearing up, but that would be a lie. It's the hypochondriac within you crying herself a river, lamenting your own fate. Why? Because you now face a merciless equation.

David Bowie burned the candle at both ends. He said: I was hitting on everybody. He was known for throwing London's best orgies, sported a fur-covered bed in the middle of his living room – furniture to sum up his philosophy. His existence was a series of too-long nights, drowned in alcohol and powdered with drugs, carried by very, very good music. And with that, a series of just as many hangovers.

But David Bowie also had specialist doctors, alternative doctors, shamans, acupuncturists, naturopaths. He had money, connections, the power to get treatment from the greatest researchers, access to technology from the future that we can't begin to imagine. He had the means to defy all logic.

This means that David Bowie can never die. Because if even he gives up the ghost, we're definitely in for it too.

You had thus far been lulled by this illusion: we could be heroes, live the present day forever, and find a remedy for eternity.

You cry, and cry. And then, that 10 January: you stop smoking.

David Bowie may just have saved your life.

AN
IDEA
OF
LOVE

He's a man you do everything secretly with. Everything but sex.

He's that man who lights a flame inside you – without actually setting your house on fire.

You send him messages that you rewrite five or six times.

You see him once a year. But think of him every day.

You sometimes share the best of yourself with him.

Wondering why you don't do it with, well, your other half.

It's irrational. You just need this secret garden.

There are films you want to see with him, but never will.

There are things you want to accomplish just to show him you're the best.

He's not in your bed, but you hear him in your head, whispering encouragement.

He has no idea how much he means to you.

He'd be very surprised.

He's the one you don't talk about, not even to your best friend.

He is this discreet, intimate place within.

He's your forbidden escape.

He's your poetic side.

You don't make love to him – because you can't make love to an idea of love.

But the good he does you is very real.

We should be allowed
to grow old twice.

The first time
we're taken by surprise.

The second,
we would have the time
to cherish time.

Things You Told Yourself You'd Never Say, Part 2

Oh, is that some new slang? What does it mean?

At twenty you think you know everything, but at my age, you realise life is a bit more complicated.

Enjoy it while it lasts – time flies.

Did you check the weather?

Don't shout, Mummy's very tired.

If I were your age, I'd do things differently.

There are plenty of fish in the sea.

We were a lost generation.

Go to the toilet before we leave. Even if you don't have to.

I don't understand anything my interns talk about.

Be a little more curious about the world around you.

I'm not wearing your Mother's Day gift because I don't want to get it dirty!

Now I avoid white wine.

If you're not hungry for your vegetables then you're not hungry for dessert.

If you swallow your chewing gum, it'll get stuck to the inside of your stomach.

I was born last century.

I think I slept with that guy. What's his name again?

Your goldfish has gone on a trip. We're not sure when he's coming back.

THE
DEAD
OF
NIGHT

Sometimes life's a bitch . . .

You used to be able to sleep whenever and wherever you wanted to, but something went off the rails and a new sly enemy emerged from the shadows: insomnia. In the dead of night, with your eyes wide open, you struggle with this unjust punishment while everyone else is in a deep sleep. You're even more annoyed that there is no one to blame for it. All you have to show for the three hours of lost sleep is a fresh wrinkle. And the next morning, you're about as cheerful as a teenager in the throes of puberty, with a brain showing early signs of dementia.

They say that pain does not treat us all equally – neither does sleep. The worst is that it starts letting you down at a point in your life when you need it most . . .

A list of your nocturnal struggles with yourself:

* **Classic Insomniac Night or *Cogito Ergo Sum:*** confirming that your brain is always working. Just a little *too* much, as the off button is supposed to be, well, off. Inevitably you turn your phone back on – everyone knows that bright screens make it ever so easy to fall back asleep.

* **In the Dead of Night:** it's 3:27 a.m., both too late and too early. You've noticed that this kind of all-nighter is often linked to lunar cycles. But when you get to work in a zombielike state and someone says 'Yeah, I hear it was a full moon – but do you actually pay attention to that nonsense?' you start to feel murderous urges from deep within that you never suspected.

* **The Morning:** no, the future doesn't always belong to those who get up early . . .

* **The First Night of Jet Lag:** when the hotel's digital clock tells you that it's 3 a.m., but your body screams that it's 6 p.m. Perfect timing . . . Your reputation and career depend on you nailing that presentation in five (four . . . three . . .) hours.

* **The Full Package:** pregnancy insomnia. Your hormones surge at night and you run to the bathroom four times. Then the baby starts to move around at dawn. This would have been the only acceptable form of insomnia, because at least you can explain it. Except that you'd been hoping to rest *before* the baby arrived. You then think of the actual process of giving birth . . . which probably won't help you get back to sleep.

You fall asleep at last, but then your alarm delivers the final blow. In that moment you fantasise about being let off the hook for the day, that everyone will treat you extra-gently, take work off your hands or just ignore you until you're over it . . . So you decide to pluck up some courage. And you send a text saying that your child has diarrhoea.

WHEN ONE
OF YOUR EYES
IS SMALLER THAN
THE OTHER.

The
New
Romantics

T here have been times in her life when she'd set out,
with clear intent and a clear objective (she's what we
call type A), and come back instead with something else
entirely, a goal, a moral or a lesson of a very different nature.

When it came to online dating – and to herself – she had long ago made up her mind: she was above all that and better than them, those people who, for want of a real social life, were reduced to liking and chatting up one another online. She'd been warned about the practices and norms:

It's a jungle out there. Ruled by narcissism, violence and volatility. Everyone knows that x is just for getting laid, but it's the same for y and z – supposedly set up for people who want more, 'a real relationship' – but they're all fronts for the same thing. You're just fresh meat, up for consumption.

But she was bored (and, *incomprehensibly,* still single). The same men always hit on her at parties, and **she'd recycled all her exes into lovers** because it was easier that way, but it had got old. And in Paris no one 'dated' – they either slept together or fell in love. Curiosity gently nagged at her.

The truth is she wanted a challenge. Taking a risk was more exciting than not experiencing anything at all. She wanted the ego boost too: with that profile photo, she'd feel like Cleopatra being discovered by wild and thirsty Romans.

* * *

She signs up for y, z and even x on a whim (and a glass of Bordeaux, which helps). Let's see which has the most appealing propositions. A one-week trial only.

The first few days unfold just how she imagined: it's a mixed bag, and she's almost shocked at who ends up trying it on. Strange to have such intimacy with strangers, even if it is virtual. But to her great surprise (and, let's be honest, disappointment), she gets very few likes . . . and when there's a rare match, and she starts up a conversation, she gets dropped along the way. What's their problem?!

When she shares the meagre findings of her digital relations with a few of her male friends, they laugh cheerfully and reveal their modus operandi: they swipe right on every profile they see. And only *then* do they select from those who opened their door.

Well, she'd only okayed three people out of the six hundred that she sifted through. She'd hesitated on the third one . . .

* * *

But here we go, her first two first dates this week.

In real life. With men who seem normal. They're not incredible, let's not get carried away, but they intrigue her.

At first with the tall, dark-haired guy, she has to force herself to smile and act relaxed. Totally out of character. But then his small talk calms her down – she realises it's good to meet regular people outside of her own circle. This conversation is unfamiliar, novel but not unpleasant: she might even start to enjoy herself. That's the moment he chooses to make a confession . . . He's not quite sure how to tell her . . . he tries again: 'Well, you see, I'm pretty old-fashioned. So, basically, I want to start a family.' As though apologising. She stifles her surprise. And though she didn't know him from Adam an hour earlier, she finds herself talking with an intimacy and honesty that she can't remember sharing with someone of the opposite sex in a long time. She lets him know that she too wants that (well, not necessarily with him, but in general).

A few days later, in another café, new guy number 2 sits across from her and cuts straight to the chase. He shows his hand almost too quickly, explaining that **he has no time to waste: if she's just looking to get laid, then she should try with someone else.** He's here to find his love match, not frolic with cyber-nymphos.

She'd gone into this to prove a sociological point: that she was too good for online daters, she was out of their league. That men were nothing but boors and womanising Casanovas, and she'd been smart to stay out of the dating game while waiting for Mr Right, for that rare pearl. But she'd discovered something else instead: there are more potential good ones out there than she'd expected, and many of them seem more romantic and confident in their wishes than many of her friends. Than even herself.

Maybe the real reason she'd still not met anyone was that she hadn't formulated and clarified what she really wanted. It is one thing to want to fall in love, but to love and build a life with someone – is that a different story?

She knows that these two men aren't necessarily representative of modern dating apps, and that her experience has been a bit unusual, and so she thinks of it as a gift. They enabled her to see how cynical she'd become. These men were sweet, they've helped her grow. They allowed her to rediscover a gentler relationship with men. Some humility too, and a welcome extra dose of romanticism.

YOU KNOW THINGS AREN'T
WHAT THEY USED TO BE

When your colleague was born the same year you graduated.

ALTERNATIVES
TO SURGERY

There are different kinds of people.

Those who praise ageing naturally, and go on about it as though you were seventy already: *'That's life!* It's beautiful to grow old, you should be proud. My grandmother has lots of wrinkles, it's wonderful to see her life story written in the lines of her face.' Yeah, sure! But you'll notice that the people who flaunt the virtues of letting nature work its magic tend to be fifteen years younger than you, they do yoga all day or have immutable genes that resist the passage of time.

Those who think we should take advantage of scientific progress and who are quite comfortable with needles and plastic surgery. 'Those droopy eyelids, they make you look like a sad puppy dog, what a waste. A nip and tuck would do the trick. Here's my surgeon's number – he's the best, he's got a magic touch. Look at me, can you even tell I've had work done?' No, not in a million years . . .

And then there are the others, a bit lost in the midst of all this, wavering between the two camps. **Dreaming of a little artificial help but completely freaked out by the thought of losing their real face** – and perhaps a bit of their soul. Those who secretly envy the smooth-skinned women with wrinkle-free foreheads they encounter on the street or in restaurants, wishing they too had the courage. But they don't. Some women and men alike do it as easily as a night out at the movies with friends, thinking it's no big deal to inject some Botox, hyaluronic acid or whatever filler. Some dermatologists even advise it from the age of twenty: 'Do it early,' they'll tell you, 'so that your wrinkles never have a chance to form!'

But at the end of the day, they can't bring themselves to take the plunge. Claiming they're worried about the health risks, though they'll swallow any pill you hand them at the first hint of a headache.

So they chase after alternative methods in their quest for eternal youth.

Because, let's face it, it's hard to watch yourself grow old.

Facial Yoga
A series of exercises that continuously works the muscles of your face.
It helps to smooth out wrinkles and restore the skin's elasticity and firmness.

The 'Pincement Jacquet' (Also acts as a Self-Massage)
Pinch some skin between your thumb and index finger in quick, rapid motions, to reach the deep muscles. It erases the lines from tired skin and adds radiance.

Diet
Raw fruits and vegetables, lemon juice in hot water in the morning and green tea give skin a healthy glow.

Kobido
An ancient Japanese massage technique that acts like a natural face-lift for the skin.
It also gives you a feeling of deep inner peace.

Oxygen Treatment

A treatment of cold oxygen blown onto your face. It improves circulation and cell regeneration, leaving skin smoother and brighter.

Cryotherapy

A treatment that uses cold air to firm up the skin and add brightness by freezing the facial nerves.
Your skin will look smoother.

Radiofrequency

A laser treatment of short waves generating heat that penetrates the soft tissue of your skin. It plumps up and tightens skin by stimulating collagen synthesis.

Aesthetic Acupuncture

A Chinese therapy that works both physically and emotionally. A method that slows down the skin's ageing process.

Single for the Long Haul

IT'S TOUGH WHEN:

- You receive birth announcements with adorable photos that make your heart swell.

- On Sunday mornings you're alone in bed, with no clue what to do with your day.

- Your love life is a taboo subject among your friends.

- Your friends suggest you follow their example. Except everybody's story is different.

- You fear you're not sharing what feels like the best years of your life with someone.

- After getting your hopes up (and putting on your sexiest lingerie), you fall asleep alone.

- Even your mum recommends you download dating apps.

- The time comes to plan your holiday, but you don't feel like travelling alone, or staying in houses full of children.

- Even P – your friend who used to be in the trenches with you – gets hitched.

IT'S EASIER WHEN:

- You realise that married life can actually be hell.

- You're free and don't have to be home by 7 p.m.

- You know that even if he were the last man on earth there is no way you'd want to sleep with P's new boyfriend.

- You receive hideous birth announcements with the tackiest designs.

- You feel as if you're making the most of the best years of your life and it feels good to be doing only what you want to do.

- You come home with someone you may never see again, but the tension is electrifying.

- You don't have to plan your holidays, because you can go wherever you want, even at the last minute.

A
POSITIVE
TWIST

Statistically speaking, you are more likely to grow old with your crew of friends than with the guy currently sharing your bed. So you need to take care of the close ones, those who are in it for life – even if they drive you crazy sometimes with their big mouths and mulelike stubbornness . . . Yes, these are your friends. So when a friendship reaches a breaking point, you have to look deep inside yourself for a very important quality: goodwill.

Warmth and kindness come with time . . . and are also a way of caring for yourself.

Some life situations:

∗ **The friend who overreacts and yells at you for something silly**
Immediate reaction: You want to ask her when she last got laid.
Goodwill reaction: You don't react to the aggressiveness, yet gently explain that her tone stung a little.

* **The friend who bails on you again**
  Immediate reaction: You tell her that you've given her countless warnings, and this was the last straw. In a rage, you hang up on her.
  Goodwill reaction: You always have a Plan B lined up when making plans with her, so you never waste an evening. Now all you have to do is figure out whether she ditched you for a date or she really is feeling down.

* **The friend who makes opposite choices from your own**
  Immediate reaction: You lose touch with her because it's too complicated to understand each other – you live on two different planets.
  Goodwill reaction: These are not easy friendships, but they help challenge us to think harder about our own opinions and, above all, to go beyond our preconceived ideas.

* **The friend who sleeps with your man**
  Immediate reaction: You hate her, you never want to see her again, you are hurt to your very core.
  Goodwill reaction: You try to understand why she did it, maybe she was just expressing insecurities about her own femininity?
  (Are you kidding? Goodwill ends when you cross that line.)

THEY TOLD
YOU IT WOULD
BE DIFFERENT
WITH TIME

(It's Not)

You pull on a swimsuit bottom when you're out of clean underwear.

You drink too much the night before a meeting that's either important or annoying, or both.

You start believing in God again whenever you need something.

You cry every time you watch *Out of Africa*, still hoping Robert Redford's plane won't take off.

You have a BFF who you love more than any of your other friends and who you won't let get away with anything.

When you watch horror movies alone in your flat, you don't dare leave your room, even just to pee, until the sun rises the next day.

You still don't know how to spell Nietzsche without checking Wikipedia first.

You still can't be bothered to make your bed in the morning. And anyway, you're also too lazy to iron your sheets.

You curse like a truck driver every time a motherfuckin' piece of shit in a car cuts you off when you're on your bike.

You still feel a longing for bad boys, even though you know to avoid them now.

You haven't read *War and Peace*, even though you pretend otherwise. And over time, you've learned to talk about it pretty convincingly.

YOU KNOW THINGS AREN'T
WHAT THEY USED TO BE

When a young woman
says she hopes
to look like you
someday.

Why
Pottery?

t was a summer day, you were about seventeen. Strolling around Paris, you came across a cobbled street and noticed an unusual shop around a corner: wilting plants hung in the window, alongside paintings of questionable taste. Pieces of wood lined the walls, dusty vases were piled up on wobbly shelves. You thought you'd found an artists' squat or a failing new-age restaurant. Through the dirty window you soon caught flashes of rippling activity: a bunch of old people, sitting on footstools, some giggling, others focused, actively spinning some unidentifiable object between their hands. Vaguely remembering your primary school art class in preparation for Father's Day, you finally concluded this was a pottery class.

Poor things, they can think of nothing better to do with them-selves, you thought. As you watched, you considered their mysterious lives: you imagined their boredom every day, the 3:33 p.m. choice among the crossword puzzle, grocery shopping and a nap. And then, *I know, let's go kill time and play with clay, with Yvonne and André!*

You gave them a final glance. You almost found the sight touching this time – their funny posture, a combination of concentration and bliss. **As you went on your way, you thought to yourself that a whole world would disappear with your parents' generation.** You were even moved to witness these last dinosaurs because one thing was certain: just like knitting or playing bridge, a century from now maybe no one would know what it was like to mould big hunks of mud.

You then forgot about this moment, like you forgot thousands of others, and you celebrated the dawn of the new millennium. Life went on.

* * *

And then. You're having lunch with an old friend who confesses she's decided to quit her job. 'Too many egos and petty politics, you know?' She wants to make a radical change in her life. She wants to dedicate herself to her true passion – but she's worried you'll judge her, because aside from being her confidante, you're also a paragon of Parisian snobbery. 'Be honest,' she says. In truth, she wants your blessing, not your opinion. Because she, one of the top editors in the literary world, has just announced that she wants to open a pottery studio.

As you respond, not only is your voice an octave higher than you intended, but there's also an irritating nasal quality to it (your panic-stricken tone betraying your true feelings). And to your own surprise you hear yourself say: 'Would you accept beginners like me?'

* * *

Proust's Madeleine . . . The memory hits you at that exact second, bitter and hard, an uppercut to the jaw. You, that once glorious young woman on a sunny street, have become a person of indeterminate age who wriggles with excitement at the prospect of handmade plates, colourful glazes and kilns.

The truth is, this idea has been on your mind for a few months now. Ever since the day you volunteered to watch your four-year-old niece during her obsessive Play-Doh phase. You couldn't leave the dining room table, even long after the child had run off some-where. Something clicked. You felt that urge to work with your hands, to plunge your fingers into that soft clay. Time stopped; the room around you disappeared. You thought about Demi Moore in *Ghost*. Pottery could be sexy. *'Oh, my love, my darling, I've hungered for your touch . . .'*

So you start your classes. You are now seated on a hassock and lovingly fondling clay. As your fingers smooth over and press into that dense paste, you start feeling unusual bursts of quasi-erotic pleasure. #potteryporn, you think. Stroking, pulling, pulp-ing, kneading and caressing. Your heartbeat slows . . . Your body relaxes . . . A sensation of warmth radiates from deep in your loins. There was no denying it, after you got to your sister's house so full of tension only to lose yourself in Play-Doh: that strange and unexpected sensation of well-being infiltrated everywhere. You are delighted – despite the ugly little ashtray wrapped in paper towels at the bottom of your purse.

* * *

You think back to that little shop, the smiling strangers through the window. You never imagined that they were collectively doing themselves good. On the verge of an orgasm. When your teenage self heard talk of 'the pleasures of age', she imagined the joys of prescription painkillers. How glad you are that she was wrong.

BITS OF WISDOM

Tips from our elders about age and the passage of time.

We've heard it from our grandmothers or their friends; we've read it in books and female celebrities' interviews: advice that is sometimes wise, sometimes strange and sometimes incomprehensible . . . advice that stuck with us or made us laugh. You might agree with this list, or not at all, so we're just going to give it to you in no particular order. Take it or leave it.

'After a certain age, a woman has to choose between her face and her arse.'

'No one will go to your grave in your place.'

'It's your life.'

'The desire to fight is truer than whatever you're fighting about.'

'The older you get, the faster time goes by.'

'You build a wall one brick at a time.'

'Age must never be an excuse for anything.'

'The more wrinkled your skin, the better ironed your clothes should be.'

'A birthday is just one more day than yesterday.'

'Toxic people should have no place in your life.'

Do not regret things you didn't do, like being crazier or having more lovers. If you didn't do them, it's because you didn't feel like it at the time and weren't ready for it. It was not you to be that way.

YOU KNOW THINGS AREN'T
WHAT THEY USED TO BE

WHEN YOU'D RATHER
GO TO BED EARLY TO
MAKE THE MOST OF
THE NEXT DAY.

'You can't help getting older,
but you don't have to
get old.'

*

—GEORGE BURNS

FOREPLAY

H is phone is on the nightstand.

He's in the shower.

Suddenly you feel an urge. You know it's wrong, you know you shouldn't . . .

But unfortunately, you know his password.

And his damn mobile phone is staring right at you, brazenly calling your name. Your hands shake, you hesitate.

You know the adage: 'If you play with fire, you get burned.' Sure, sure. You also know that every time you snooped around on someone else's mobile phone, you found something to stoke the flames, your heart missed a few beats – or even shattered into a million pieces.

So what to do? You try diving back into your book, but it's too late. You start to panic. Opportunities like this don't come around that often – what if you miss your chance? You listen closely to analyse the bathroom noises. Pragmatic as ever, you determine that you have about two minutes to get cracking on your shameful search. Your fingers are about to type in the passcode. But. BUT.

In the span of a second, it all plays out in your mind like a film on fast-forward:

* As you type in the code, your heart would beat so fast you'd be on the verge of a fit.

* You'd start by scrawling through the messages, the texts, the WhatsApp . . .

* You'd identify unfamiliar names.

* You'd look for the unusual messages, trying to recall where you were that night.

* And that's when you'd read something that will punch you in the gut.

* It would feel like a high. A violent rush of adrenaline.

* It would be that pain that you were seeking, that pain you craved, without knowing why.

* From a few cryptic words, you'd picture different scenarios.

* You'd feel sad and betrayed.

* You'd burst into the bathroom, screaming, brandishing his phone.

* You'd yell, cry, threaten.

* There'd be hours of arguing, hours of drama and sulking.

In the bathroom, the shower stops. Whether you're being paranoid, whether or not this is true, you realise you know this story by heart and proudly put the phone down.

LIVING
EFFORTLESSLY

For every problem there's a pill. That's been your motto and it hasn't changed since your tender years. When you were twenty you popped Ecstasy to cure the shyness keeping you from wild dancing and making out with hot strangers. For the next few years you swapped birth control for morning-after pills (because sometimes you'd forget to take the former, obviously). You then started with weight-loss pills and their promise of magically melting away winter fat without lifting a finger. Disappointed, you headed into your holiday with loaded suitcases and excess baggage on your thighs. And yet – your faith in magic pills was unshakeable.

Next came dietary supplements – everything you ever dreamed of was in those bottles. Feeling short-tempered, annoyed by everything and everyone, including yourself? Say no more – magnesium, twice a day. You keep forgetting things? Omega-3, as much as you like: improves your memory and your concentration. Hair thinning? Brewer's yeast, with breakfast and dinner.

Years went by, faster and faster. You concocted mixtures like a mad scientist, creating explosions of strange and wonderful molecules. Your pillbox got heavier than your grandma's and you knew you'd soon be eating sugar-coated tablets for dinner every night. The results were more or less convincing. It crossed your mind you might be stuffing yourself with placebos, but who cares? **You needed pills, pills and more pills to reassure yourself.** Everything will be okay. Your attitude was over the top, you were making yourself sick trying to control everything with a science that is not always exact.

And then one day the real diagnosis hits you: your true affliction in life is, actually, a terrible lack of willpower. You want these magical pills to fix your problems at the snap of a finger. You want the pleasure of success without the pain of the slightest effort.

You let this truth sink in.

And a second later you ask yourself:

Where's the pill for that?

Mother
and Son

L was comfortable with her online presence.

She had joined Instagram, with a few strict self-imposed guidelines: not to post photos of herself (there's an age limit to selfies) and not to flood everyone with family pictures (seriously, *no one* gives a shit). As a result, she limited her posts to landscapes, cultural tips and design ideas. She had found a kind of equilibrium and several hundred followers, mainly people of a similar mind-set. And so she was able to spend hours indulging in perfect voyeurism, following strangers without subjecting her own face and ego to their judgement. She thought she was safe from any online misadventures. Until the day one of her friends, with a bit of a smirk, asked her what she thought of the big news.

'What news?'

'Your son's new girlfriend.'

' . . . '

'You didn't see the photo?'

This exchange introduced L to something irrational: Her son, her little boy, not only had a girlfriend but also his very own Instagram account. An account that she didn't know about, but onto which he had accepted one of *her* friends. So this friend now had access to a secret aspect of her son's life. She wanted to cry. Fortunately, she managed to contain herself. She knew she was being childish and overreacting, but she still felt excluded. Then she reasoned with herself: a child's privacy has to be respected. Even when they decide out of nowhere to cut the cord with their bare teeth.

She went back home, sat down in her living room with a book, and waited for her eldest son to return. When he did, she looked up at him and said:

'I didn't know you had an account.'

'What?'

'Instagram.'

'Yeah.'

'I'm going to follow you then.'

'No. If you do, I'm going to have to ignore your request.'

Bam. Unexpected uppercut. The blow hurt. Banned from his world.

The following days, L thought a lot about the account, about her child's life, which was passing by right under her nose. She wondered whether she'd made a mistake. She had thought of herself as the cool mum you could tell anything to. But most of all, L thought about the friend of hers who had the right to access this restricted zone.

At home, she barely spoke to her eldest son. Not that she was truly angry with him, but it was so difficult for her to broach the subject that she found it easier to stay quiet. She was afraid that as soon as she opened her mouth, the word *Instagram* would slip out like a burp. Her younger son seemed worried about the strange atmosphere that had taken over the flat. All three of them were sitting at the table one night for dinner. The eldest son stared at his mother as they ate pasta. He sighed.

'It's fine.'

'What?'

'I'll accept your request.'

'I didn't ask you to . . .'

He rolled his eyes, got up, and went to his room. Alone with her younger son, L wondered what was taking so long. She got out her phone, refreshed the page of her follow request over and over. Nothing. Her son shook his head.

'Wait a little.'

'Why?'

'He's cleaning it up.'

'Deleting things?'

'*Obviously.*'

L was boiling. She wanted to burst into her son's room. She didn't want to force her son to show her this part of his private life. She wanted him to *want* to share it, of his own accord, with the woman who had brought him into the world.

The eldest son returned and sat back down at the table.

'All right, I added you.'

'I know that you deleted some of the photos.'

' . . . '

'You know what, this is a good litmus test. A photo that you can't show your mother is a photo you should probably not be posting.'

' . . . '

'You know, whatever you post online is going to follow you for a long, long time.'

'Mum.'

'What?'

'I'm eighteen years old.'

YOU KNOW THINGS AREN'T
WHAT THEY USED TO BE

WHEN YOU FIND YOURSELF PUTTING ON MAKEUP EVERY DAY.

THE GOOD FIT

The one who's not a total square.

The glasses may be see-through, but she's not.

She's broadening her horizons.

The nerd who wants to change the world. Gandhi is my master.

Marguerite Duras.

There are many different sides to her.

She's got big ones too.

Subliminal glasses: make it clear that you're the rare pearl.

STEPKIDS

The French word for stepmother is *belle-mère,* which means 'beautiful mother'. A tad hypocritical? Well . . . this role can sometimes be truly rewarding and have its redeeming moments. But sometimes you're ready to throw it all out the window – the kids . . . and their father with them!

Mixed feelings:

* Hearing: 'You're not my mother!'

* The secrets they share with you because you're not their father.

* To have your favourite sweater 'borrowed' despite hiding it at the back of the wardrobe.

* Their mother, who does everything so much better than you do.

* When you realise you think of them as your own kids.

* Finding them worse behaved than your own would be (if you had any).

* When you try in vain to charm them and win them over, when what you should be doing is helping them grow and move forward.

* The pride you feel when you're so close you could be mistaken for mother and daughter.

* Explaining that they should not speak disrespectfully to you just because you're not their mother.

* The little things they do for you – when you least expect it.

* The fact that they'll forget you the moment you're no longer with their father. But that one day, years after the split, they'll tell you that you matter.

Growing Up

A s a teen, it all seemed crystal clear: you'd be an adult when you turned twenty-eight.

You chose twenty-eight, a serious-sounding even number, partly by the process of elimination: it was older than twenty-five, the symbolic quarter of a century and the last arguably 'young' birthday; you'd no longer be a student; you'd be independent, having obviously left the family nest; you'd finally be free of those prepubescent love affairs; and it was around the right age to start thinking about children.

But above all, you would be past the age when your parents and older siblings could exploit you for free. You would have a real job with a pay cheque – and with any luck, people would listen to you and follow your advice. In short, you would exist for and thanks to yourself. And even the idea of having your driver's licence and being alone in a car – what an accomplishment that would be!

All of this would surely come to pass in that promised land of twenty-eight, the land where people would trust you, where you wouldn't need permission to stay out all night, where you could rent a car and drive off somewhere on a whim. Where you could basically do what you wanted to whenever you wanted to: sleep, drink, do drugs and spend your money as you wished.

In other words: you wouldn't have to answer to anyone ever again. True freedom.

* * *

Twenty-eight years old and then some:

It was time to face the facts. **Maybe you were technically grown-up now in the sense that people called you Madam instead of Miss,** but you still felt like a child waiting on the steps at the pearly gates of adulthood.

No driver's licence, for starters. Your assortment of odd jobs barely covered the rent for your studio, and the career you were dreaming of was nowhere in sight. Maybe in part due to your phobia of paperwork and refusal to open your emails. Yes, that must be it. Your latest romantic endeavours didn't have a leg up on your old high-school flames. You didn't understand commitment any more than you did hookup culture. You gave mixed signals and got rejections in return.

Everything had started out so well – at what point did it unravel?

Ironically, in your early twenties you had been responsible, too serious almost. You were determined to check off all the obligatory rites of passage that would lead you to your cherished freedom: you needed to do well in school, find a job and not disappoint your parents. You woke up at dawn like a modern woman, you kept your mouth shut when the mediocre higher-ups at your company stole your good ideas, and you even managed to fill out your tax forms with some accuracy, proudly contributing to society – at least symbolically. At your first-ever solo housewarming party in that gloomy flat, surrounded by friends who all had sleep deprivation stamped under their eyes, evidence of their low-paying jobs, you asked yourself: **Am I an adult now? Is this it?**

So when you reached thirty, you decided to turn it all on its head. You didn't owe anything to anyone, wouldn't get married and have a kid just like everyone else. You would dive into the exact opposite of what everyone expected, smoking all night and playing online poker – knowing full well that it would take you nowhere, and you'd probably end up with yellow skin and lung cancer as a bonus. You ate junk food and ignored the dishes piling up in the sink. You stopped answering your parents' worried texts, you blocked your bank manager's number to keep her quiet, you took a chance on some of the wilder guys, just to see what would happen.

Besides, don't people say that 'forty is the new thirty'? You wanted to live in the moment, to stop chasing pipe dreams and enjoy each day as it came. **And what if being grown-up also means deciding to be irresponsible – allowing yourself to misbehave every now and then?**

In reality, those transitional years in your thirties gave you a chance to take stock of everyone around you. Everything started coming slowly into focus until the truth was staring right back at you. All those people who were pretending to know what they were doing, adopting a serious expression to talk about things that they barely understood: they were children in adult clothing. With makeup. And suits. And mature haircuts. And multisyllable adult words. All of it was make-believe. You've seen it when elderly people calmly cut in front of you at the supermarket: they simply don't feel like pretending anymore, and they don't have to. They finally dare to let the mask fall.

Adulthood, you've finally understood, is always just a little bit later than now.

Being a grown-up is for tomorrow.

TEN
YEARS
YOUNGER

At school, every French girl learns Pierre de Ronsard's poem that begins, 'See, Mignonne, hath not the Rose . . .' It's the story of a poet in love with a young woman who doesn't return his affections. Despondent and bitter, he suggests that the girl come look at the roses in his garden. They take a stroll among the flowers, each more beautiful than the next. But at the end, the poet shows the young girl that the roses fade very quickly, warning her that one day, she too will be old and ugly like a wilted flower. And then she'll regret not giving herself to the poet 'in the flower of your youth'. In short, old Ronsard seeks revenge as best he can. **And we girls learn from an early age that the beauty of our youth is fleeting and we will need to prepare for our retirement.** So because of lecherous Ronsard – or maybe thanks to him – we already know as eight-year-olds that there's no point in trying to fight Time: that bastard will always win. But since we're so prepared for what's to come, we have plenty of time to figure out what to do. And maybe that's one of the reasons people say that Frenchwomen age well. They're not obsessed with youth – they know that's a losing battle from the start – but rather with the idea of looking a bit younger than they are. A difference that might seem subtle, but is very important!

In keeping with her mantra 'Enjoy the face you have today – it's the one you'll wish you have ten years from now,' **the French-woman cares not about looking twenty, but about looking ten years younger than she is.** And without hiding her real age. For she loves to reveal how old she is, to savour the effect it will have on her listener. 'Seriously? No way!' (Some even go so far as to add a couple of extra years, just for the pleasure of seeming even younger.) The art of looking ten years younger is a national sport in France, and we're always trying to improve our technique and hone our skills – without looking like we're trying, obviously.

Here are a few tips to help you develop this sophisticated art:

* Choose fitted clothing (shirts, jackets) and fabrics rather than loose cuts (T-shirts, sweaters). Or mix it up: wear a loose T-shirt under a fitted jacket.

* A white shirt – a bit masculine, cotton or linen – is always the right move.

* An impeccable T-shirt that shows off your neck and collarbone. But careful with the cleavage. Hinting – not showing – is always more enticing.

* Showing an insatiable curiosity will make you look younger than a new pair of breasts.

* Take care of your extremities: your hands (and fingernails), your feet (and shoes) and your head (and hair).

* The most important thing is your complexion. So spend time perfecting it – then a swipe of mascara and you're all done.

* For photos: smile! It's cuter than a pout. And laugh whenever you can – it pulls the rest of your face up, like a natural face-lift.

* Stop smoking. Your skin will thank you.

* Spend less time staring at yourself in the mirror. Spend more time looking at others.

* Read books – but no Pierre de Ronsard!

* For a good complexion, you need impeccable skin. Take off your makeup every night. Even when you're not wearing any makeup.

* It's all a question of attitude, not the tightness of your skin. Youth is as much about freedom and joy as it is about firm thighs.

* Continue to be curious about anyone and everything.

* One glass of good wine is better than several shots of bad vodka.

* Get out of the sun and invest in a cap and a good sunscreen. They're cheaper and more effective than restorative creams that cost as much as caviar.

* Being extremely thin makes your skin look dull, tired and stretched. There's no point in being too thin, as you risk looking ten years older.

* A deep-tissue facial massage staves off the need for a face-lift. Parisian women whisper their best technicians' contact info among themselves. It's the secret to their beauty, and a long-term investment. A massage a month keeps the plastic surgeon away.

* Take care of your eyebrows. Don't pluck too much, but don't let the garden grow wild either.

* Watch out for sugar, whether it's in alcohol, sweets or fizzy drinks. Sugar pulls on your features and gives you a tired look.

* Take a close look at your mother. Identify the flaws and work on them.

Things You Survived, Eventually

- Unrequited love.

- Giving birth.

- And then the first months of your child's life.

- Sending a text in which you criticised a friend, to that friend, who probably wasn't a real friend.

- A burnout – which almost has become a necessary rite of passage to guarantee a fulfilling career.

- Your divorce.

- Extreme solitude.

- Quitting smoking.

- The tattooed initials of someone you now remember nothing about, except their initials.

- The end of your favourite series.

Places in Paris Where Time Stands Still

HOTELS

**A little bit of
countryside in Paris**
HÔTEL DES GRANDES ÉCOLES
75 Rue du Cardinal Lemoine,
Paris 05

A manor from 1870
HÔTEL LANGLOIS
63 Rue Saint-Lazare, Paris 09

Facing the Tuileries Garden (1900)
HÔTEL RÉGINA
2 Place des Pyramides, Paris 01

**A traditional
nineteenth-century hotel**
HÔTEL CHOPIN
46 Passage Jouffroy, Paris 09

RESTAURANTS

THE Parisian Brasserie
BRASSERIE LIPP
151 Boulevard Saint-Germain,
Paris 06

Michelin star 1930s brasserie
LA POULE AU POT
9 Rue Vauvilliers, Paris 01

Traditional French cuisine
LE PETIT SAINT BENOIT
4 Rue Saint-Benoit, Paris 06

Restaurant est. 1896
BOUILLON CHARTIER
7 Rue du Faubourg
Montmartre, Paris 09

Large terrace in the heart
of Buttes Chaumont park
PAVILLON PUEBLA
Parc des Buttes Chaumont,
Avenue Darcel, Paris 19

A restaurant at the train
station (1900)
LE TRAIN BLEU
Gare de Lyon, Place
Louis-Armand,
Paris 12

Gourmet bistro (1900)
LE CHARDENOUX
1 Rue Jules Vallès,
Paris 11

Old-world bistro
LE VERRE À PIED
118 Rue Mouffetard,
Paris 05

Legendary Chinese restaurant
LE PRESIDENT
120 Rue du Faubourg du Temple,
Paris 11

Post-concert restaurant
AU BOEUF COURONNÉ
188 Avenue Jean Jaurès,
Paris 19

The best couscous
in a 1930s décor
CHEZ OMAR
47 Rue de Bretagne,
Paris 03

Historic seafood brasserie
LE WEPLER
14 Place de Clichy,
Paris 18

Japanese restaurant in
a 1900-era bistro
KUNITORAYA 2
5 Rue Villédo,
Paris 01

CAFÉS

Typical Saint-Germain bar
LE ROUQUET
188 Boulevard Saint-Germain,
Paris 07

Café a short walk from the
Luxembourg Gardens
CAFÉ FLEURUS
2 Rue de Fleurus,
Paris 06

Belle epoque tearoom
ANGELINA
226 Rue de Rivoli,
Paris 01

Japanese pastry shop
and café
TORAYA
10 Rue Saint-Florentin,
Paris 01

Jazzy flea-market hangout
LA CHOPE DES PUCES
122 Rue des Rosiers,
Saint-Ouen

BARS

Thirties jazz mood
ROSEBUD
11 Rue Delambre, Paris 14

Hundred-year-old
New York–style bar
HARRY'S NEW YORK BAR
5 Rue Daunou, Paris 02

Fifties bar
CHEZ CAMILLE
8 Rue Ravignan, Paris 18

Swing dance hall
LE CAVEAU DE LA HUCHETTE
5 Rue de la Huchette, Paris 05

SHOPPING

A perfumery and pharmacy
for natural beauty products
OFFICINE UNIVERSELLE
BULY 1803
6 Rue Bonaparte, Paris 06

The most chic ceramics
in Paris
ASTIER DE VILLATTE
173 Rue Saint-Honoré,
Paris 01

Fine art bookstore
LIBRAIRIE DE NOBELE
3 Rue Bonaparte,
Paris 06

English-language bookstore and library
SHAKESPEARE & COMPANY
37 Rue de la Bûcherie,
Paris 05

Shopping in a covered passage (1826)
GALERIE VÉRO-DODAT
19 Rue Jean-Jacques Rousseau,
Paris 01

Vintage jewellery
DARY'S
362 Rue Saint-Honoré,
75001 Paris

Antiques flea market
LE MARCHÉ VERNAISON
99 Rue des Rosiers,
Saint-Ouen

The temple of all fabrics since 1920
MARCHÉ SAINT PIERRE
2 Rue Charles Nodier,
Paris 18

Middle Eastern and Asian supermarket
IZRAËL
30 Rue François Miron,
Paris 04

Typically Parisian market for vegetables (1921)
MARCHÉ MONGE
1 Place Monge,
Paris 05

Covered food market (1843)
MARCHÉ BEAUVAU
Place d'Aligre, Paris 12

Food products from Auvergne
CHEZ TEIL
6 Rue de Lappe, Paris 11

Retro pastry shop
LES PETITS MITRONS
26 Rue Lepic, Paris 18

Chocolate
À LA MÈRE DE FAMILLE
35 Rue du Faubourg
Montmartre, Paris 09

TO DO

Eighties swimming pool
PISCINE PAILLERON
32 Rue Edouard Pailleron,
Paris 19

A massage in the Parisian skies
LADDA
32 Rue de Paradis, Paris 10

Movie theatre from the twenties
LE LOUXOR
170 Boulevard de Magenta,
Paris 10

Independent art-house theatre
CHRISTINE 21
4 Rue Christine, Paris 06

A ballet at the opera
PALAIS GARNIER
Place de l'Opéra, Paris 09

**Hispano-Moorish-style Mosque
(1922–1926)
LA GRANDE MOSQUÉE
DE PARIS**
2 bis Place du Puits de l'Ermite,
Paris 05

**Painter Gustave Moreau's studio
MUSÉE GUSTAVE MOREAU**
14 Rue de la Rochefoucauld,
Paris 09

**Sculptor Antoine Bourdelle's
apartment
MUSÉE BOURDELLE**
18 Rue Antoine Bourdelle,
Paris 15

**The Parisian student's
library (1851)
BIBLIOTHÈQUE SAINTE
GENEVIEVE**
10 Place du Panthéon, Paris 05

**Reproduction of sculptor
Constantin Brâncuși's studio
ATELIER BRÂNCUŞI**
Place Georges Pompidou,
Paris 04

ACKNOWLEDGEMENTS

Thanks to Shelley Wanger, Susanna Lea, Mark Kessler, Bette Alexander, Pei Loi Koay, Naja Baldwin, Christian Bragg and Johan Lindeberg at BLK DNM.

Angloma, Camille Arnaud, Joseph Belingard, Yoan Benzaquen at Marc Le Bihan, the Berest family, Diane Carcassonne, Chanel, Philippe Cerboneschi, Diana Chen, the Chertok family, Rhizlaine El Cohen, Laurent Fetis, Guy Fischer, Saraï Fiszel, Françoise Gavalda, Kerry Glencorse, Clémentine Goldszal, Honorine Goueth, Alizée Guinochet, Sébastien Haas, Raphaël Hamburger, Lubna Karmitz, Ladda Paris, Yaël Langmann, Rémi de Laquintane, Magdalena Lawniczak, Marc Le Bruchec, Zen and Akiro Lefort, the Lefort family, Marc-Edouard Léon, Saif Mahdhi at Safe Management, Stéphane Manel, Tessa Manel, the Mas family, Jules and Arthur Mas, Amanda Messenger, Judith Meyerson, Jacqueline Ngo Mpii, Priscille d'Orgeval, Ryan Ouimet, Lorenzo Païno Fernandez, Bertrand Le Pluard, Natalie Portman, Anton Poupaud, Yarol Poupaud, Elsa Rakotoson, Anne and Fabrice Roger-Lacan, Joachim Roncin, Xavier de Rosnay, Lourenço Sant' Anna, Céline Savoldelli, Sou Sinuvong, Rodrigo Teixeira, Alix Thomsen, Claire Tran, Camille Vizzavona, Studio Zéro, Rébecca Zlotowski.

CONTENTS

Mind Yourself

Love Eventually

Just Saying

The Great Escape

Beauty Call

ILLUSTRATION CREDITS